EXCHANGE THE TRUTH FOR A LIE

EXCHANGE THE TRUTH FOR A LIE

DECEPTION AND THE HARD HEART

RICK THOMAS

EXCHANGE THE TRUTH FOR A LIE:
Deception and the Hard Heart

ISBN 978-1-7323854-9-8

Rick Thomas

© 2025 Life Over Coffee

Unless otherwise noted, all Scripture references herein are from the English Standard Version, copyright © 2001 by Crossway, Inc. Used by permission. All rights reserved.

No part of this publication may be reproduced, stored in a retrieval system, or transmitted in any form or by any means without the express written permission of Life Over Coffee.

Edited by Sarah Hayhurst

Life Over Coffee
8595 Pelham Rd Ste 400 #406,
Greenville, SC 29615
LifeOverCoffee.com

Therefore God gave them up in the lusts of their hearts to impurity, to the dishonoring of their bodies among themselves, because they exchanged the truth about God for a lie and worshiped and served the creature rather than the Creator, who is blessed forever! Amen.

(Romans 1:24–25)

For additional resources, visit

lifeovercoffee.com

Table of Contents

    Introduction 8
1. Exchange the Truth 10
2. Walk Away from the Faith 20
3. Steps to a Hard Heart 30
4. When I Was Silent 38
5. My Friend's Sin Secret 48
6. Reasons for No Change 58
7. Expecting Change 66
8. A Better Way 76
9. Forcing Change 86
10. Consider This 94
11. Four Steps to Change 104
12. Marks of Change 114
    Conclusion 122
    About the Author 124

Introduction

This book is for all of us because it speaks to our shared human condition. "Today, if you hear His voice, do not harden your heart" is the clarion warning from the Book of Hebrews. What was said two millennia ago is just as relevant today. Life in a fallen world can be a ruthless and dangerous place. The race we began has more twists and turns than we could have imagined. Every person's temptation is to draw back, give up, walk away, and create a new kind of truth. To walk with Jesus is a death walk, which sounds less demanding when read from the Bible than when lived out daily. Shifting back from a cross-carrying life begins in invisible ways—a gradient journey with thousands of micro-decisions. You may not even recognize your drifting from the truth of God.

This book can re-calibrate your soul while transforming your life with others in God's world. It won't be easy. Through these pages, you will see how God has effectively appropriated His grace in your life, but there will be other areas where you'll "hear His voice," appealing to you not to exchange His truth for a lie. If there is any sense of the LORD's conviction as you read, I appeal to you to stop and zero in on those areas where change is needed. At the end of each chapter, I have call-to-action opportunities for you to self-reflect and assess. Take time to do this. Here are a few ways you can make the most of this book:

Introduction

1. Read prayerfully and expectantly as you move from page to page.
2. Journal your thoughts. Don't casually pass or dismiss the ah-ha moments. You're not in a race to finish. The sanctification is a process, as much as it can be a series of events.
3. Take your time. Perhaps your device allows you to highlight sentences and make notes inside the book. Go for it.
4. Take your thoughts to the LORD. Ask Him to help you see what you can't see.
5. Finally, share what you are learning with a friend. The teacher will always learn more than the student, and if you share your sanctification reflections, you will begin to own them.

I pray that God will call many people back to their first love while others find the motivation to make ever-so-slight changes in their lives through the sweet applications of God's eternal truths. It is a joy to serve you. I'm so glad that you're reading this book. May the LORD of all keep you abiding in His truth while mercifully guarding you against the dangerous exchange.

Rick

1

Exchange the Truth

Have you ever wondered what happens to a person who exchanges the truth of God for a lie? Perhaps you know someone who has made this troubling exchange. They were once walking in the truth of God's Word, but now they have created a new reality—their truth, which conflicts with God's truth, placing the "exchanger" in the unenviable position of going to war with God. Paul talked about this in Romans 1:21-25. Let me share with you what happens to such a person.

Truth Suppressors

Anytime we switch from adhering to God's truth to clinging to an alternate fluid reality, we can expect a process of "soul degradation." Paul was talking about a group of people who knew God, but for reasons that are not entirely clear, they decided to walk away from Him, choosing instead to worship and serve the creature more than the Creator. From that point of departure from God, things became progressively worse for them. Their lives became a slow march of deterioration of body and soul. We know why: God was pressing down His wrath on them.

> For the wrath of God is revealed from heaven against all ungodliness and unrighteousness of men, who by their unrighteousness suppress the truth.
> (Romans 1:18)

Paul writes about the displeasure of God raining down from heaven on any person who chooses to push His truth out of their lives. This passage applies to all of us, not just the determined sinners who actively and angrily suppress the truth of God out of their lives. Paul tells us about a universal, absolute cause and effect regardless of how big or nasty the sin is. He is saying the displeasurable wrath of God automatically descends from on high when a person chooses to sin, whether it's a cute toddler or the hardened criminal. Paul uses the language of "suppressing the truth" of God out of their lives, which means pushing aside God's truth—a voluntary choice to ignore what is right.

In verse 21, he talks about how nobody has an excuse for pushing the truth of God out of their lives. He further expands on this idea in Romans 2:14–15 when he talks about the non-believing Gentiles who do not have the Bible but know how to do the things contained in the Bible. Knowing the truth is not the exclusive domain of the religious person. It does not matter who you are or how much you know about God; none of us can get away with using excuses when responding incorrectly to God. We all are without defenses (Romans 1:20).

Opposing God

> But he gives more grace. Therefore it says, "God opposes the proud but gives grace to the humble."
> (James 4:6)

For whatever reason, some people choose to alter God's truth into a truth that is more aligned with their preferences. When they do this, they set themselves up for a displeasurable response from God. I have seen this in my life. For example, the "so-called" most minor sin in my marriage puts me in an adversarial position with God (and my wife). He is no longer "for me" regarding my sanctification (1 John 1:7–10). Though I can never lose my salvation, I can impede our relational well-being when I choose to do my thing. This pushing of God's truth out of my life also interrupts the shalom in our marriage.

We cannot sin and expect things to be okay between ourselves and the people with whom we sinned. God's Word is true: we push His truth out of our lives, and we'll incur His wrath. I often use a weenie balloon illustration when describing Romans 1:18. It goes like this: the idea of suppressing the truth or pushing it out of your life is analogous to squeezing a weenie balloon full of air. The balloon becomes exaggerated on each end as soon as you press it in the middle. You cannot put pressure on the center without the ends being affected.

The balloon becomes out-of-balance, and so does our lives when we push the truth of God's Word out of our lives. We become awkward with God and awkward with others. We're no longer in step with what is right (Galatians 2:14). When God's displeasure comes into our lives because we chose to reject His truth, we cannot help but live an awkward, out-of-balance life. We cannot be *Jesus-normal* when God is standing in opposition to us. I describe this concept with this mindmap, and analytical teaching tool I use to assist friends in visualizing spiritual concepts.

Exchange the Truth

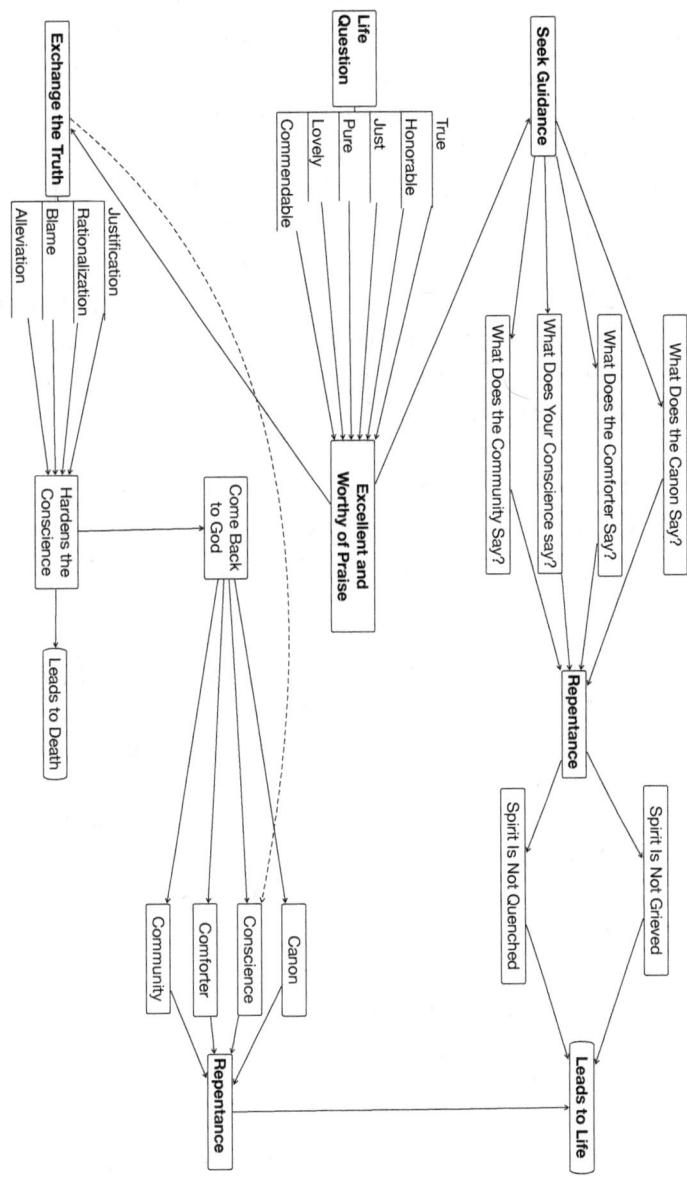

Mapping Our Decisions

You can visually see what I am talking about in the mindmap. The process goes from left to right. The individual is thinking about a life question, e.g., how I want to live in God's world. The first step in that process is to run their thoughts through the Philippians 4:8 filter. You can do this by asking yourself a series of questions:

- Is this thing I want to do true, honorable, just, pure, lovely, and commendable?
- If it is all of these things, is it worthy of praise and an excellent thing to do?

If the person is unsure how to answer these questions biblically, it would be wise to reach out for help. They can access the four means of grace we are given from the Bible to make sound decisions:

- What does the Bible (Canon) say about what I want to do?
- What does the Spirit (Comforter) say about what I want to do?
- What does my inner voice (conscience) say about what I want to do?
- What does the body of Christ (community) say about what I want to do?

After seeking sound advice from these four means of grace and believing there are no reasons to halt, the person should be able to proceed in faith, knowing the Lord's favor is on their lives because they were not trying to push their agenda. However, some folks want to do what they want, regardless of what God and others think about their choices. If that is their response, you want to consider at least these five possible reasons they reject God and sound advice.

Progression into Darkness

1. They are angry at God, and they no longer care about what is right or wrong. (Perhaps disappointment is a better synonym for anger; disappointment is a form of anger.)
2. Next, they did something impulsively, not thinking about right or wrong, and they are unwilling to return and make things right.
3. They make half-hearted attempts to keep from yielding to an ongoing temptation, but they decided to give up and go their way (Proverbs 14:12).
4. They resign, thinking they have always been the way they are and have never known any other way to live—so they go with it.
5. They sinned and liked it; they don't want to let go of it, and the habituation forms.

Regardless of how they got to the point of their lousy lifestyle choice, they prefer to stick with their poor choice rather than do the hard thing, which is to die to themselves and walk with the Lord (Mark 8:34). The call to die is much harder at first glance than the desire to do your thing; so, they do what they want to do. At this decisive point, the individual has begun exchanging the truth of God for a lie, though they have not exchanged it entirely. But they are well on their way to the dark side. Let's review what has happened thus far in chronological order of their micro-decisions:

1. They wanted to do something; perhaps it was a lifestyle choice.
2. They analyzed whether it was the right thing to do.
3. They may or may not have sought help in their decision-making.
4. They decided to push the truth (suppress) of God out of their lives.

5. God is no longer for them (Romans 8:31).
6. His wrath begins to rain down from heaven against them (Romans 1:18).
7. They are warring with God (James 4:6).
8. Their minds begin the process of turning futile and dark (Ephesians 4:17–19).
9. The path to disobedience has begun.
10. They are making themselves "okay" with the truth exchange.
11. Next stop: desensitization to the truth of God.

Muting the Inner Voice

> For when Gentiles, who do not have the law, by nature do what the law requires, they are a law to themselves, even though they do not have the law. They show that the work of the law is written on their hearts, while their conscience also bears witness, and their conflicting thoughts accuse or even excuse them.
>
> (Romans 2:14–15)

Paul talked about how our souls churn inside us when our consciences struggle with God's morality. Any decision to do the wrong thing does not mitigate the "noise" that is going on in our souls. Just because we decided to do what is wrong does not mean our struggle between right and wrong has subsided. Even the unregenerate conscience fights the battle with soul noise. Though the person has suppressed God's truth from his life, his conscience is still active and responding to his wrong choice. The only way for him to get rid of his sin is by repentance, but if that is not the choice he makes, he must begin a process of re-scripting his conscience so he can fully exchange the truth of God for a lie and live with himself at the same time.

With the Canon sitting on the self, the Comforter turned

down low to where the Spirit no longer illuminates his mind, and his dismissing of community, the last thing for him to do is shut the conscience down so he does not have to hear its voice pinging him at every turn. There are four ways for him to alter his conscience to push God's truth entirely out of his life successfully. When finished, he will be able to do whatever it is he wants to do without feeling. Those four things are:

- Justify his actions, declaring himself "not guilty" of any wrongdoing.
- Rationalize his actions by comparing his life to others—a means of excusing himself from liability.
- Blaming his actions on other people or specific events in his life.
- Alleviating any discomfort he may feel, which "medicates" the mind with a new truth—his truth.

Call to Action

Since repentance is out of the question, he has no choice but to turn to these four noise reducers to live in his version of the truth. Once that is complete, he successfully exchanged God's truth for a lie, which is no man's land. It is flying blind in a storm. It is the worst possible place for any human to be. God is not with him, for him, or helping him. His mind is evolving into darkness. He is becoming desensitized to the truth. He has set aside the people who can help him the most. He is on his own.

1. For those of you *going dark*: if you are making these choices, let this appeal be your warning and guide. Don't choose the four ways—justify, rationalize, blame, alleviate—of making your life choices "okay" when it is not okay for you to live that way.

Choose repentance. You can do that by letting someone know what is happening with you. Begin to change today.
2. For those of you who *are dark*: if the light is off, you've made your bed, and you have no plans to change your lifestyle, let this be your warning. You can do what you want, but please be aware that God has stern warnings for those who persist in their ways—especially if you call yourself a Christian.
3. For those of you who *know a dark soul*: if you know of someone trying to exchange the truth of God for a lie, please warn them by any means that is appropriate. To be desensitized to the truth of God is as precarious as you can be. If you can, please speak the truth in love to them. You're welcome to use what I have said here to come alongside those you care for and love.

Exchange the Truth

2

Walk Away from the Faith

Can a Christian walk away from God? To help work through this question, we must first recognize and accept that Christianity is not neat, and sin has never been respectful of our preferred categories. We also have to admit that this conversation is subjective in nature: we cannot know what is happening in a person's heart or all the ancillary issues that contribute to why a person would "accept and reject" Christ. The Hebrew writer is suggesting there can be this kind of Christian—a believer who spurns the grace he once received for whatever reasons. What does that mean? How are we to think about friends who reject Christ?

Lost or Found

I recently counseled a man addicted to sin. He was living a self-centered, self-serving lifestyle that kept Christ from ruling his heart (Colossians 3:16). It was not that long ago when he professed Christ. Then he made a sinful choice to love his sin, which became a controlling preference that now dominates him (Romans 1:2; Galatians 6:1). Of course, there are a few people who know him who have said that he was never saved: "He made a profession, but he did not have the possession of Christ." It fits nicely on a bumper sticker.

A person can indeed acknowledge the facts about Christ while not possessing the transforming power of the gospel (Romans 12:1-2). This problem has been called intellectual assent—a person giving consent to the truth claims of the gospel but not experiencing regeneration by them (John 3:1-7). I suppose that many people are Christianized but not truly transformed (Matthew 7:21). What if we spent some time wrestling through this subjective truth about some of our friends who love their sin more than Christ? Perhaps starting with a few questions would help.

- Can not being a Christian be the only answer for my friend?
- Is there only one category for a person who persists in a sinful lifestyle while tacitly hanging around the Christian community?
- Can a person walk away from genuine faith?
- How do you make sense of a person who once walked with Christ but has since fallen away?
- Is there any responsibility on the believer regarding the perseverance of the saints?

Not Mincing Words

In the book of Hebrews, what does the call to hold fast to your salvation mean if the interpretation is not for us to hold on to our faith? No doubt, God perseveres for you (primary cause), but aren't you supposed to cooperate with Him (secondary cause) by persisting in your sanctification? The Hebrew writer observed his brothers and sisters turning and walking away from their faith, and he did not mince words but gave stern warnings to those who did not want to follow the Savior anymore.

The writer was willing and able to live in the theological tension of "for by grace you are saved" (Ephesians 2:8-9) and "you must hold fast to your confession of faith" (Hebrews

10:23). Here are some of the most explicit passages in Hebrews that speak to our call for active obedience. Read and reflect upon these passages. Think through primary and secondary causes. Do you see God's perseverance and our responsibility to hold on? How do you reconcile those two seemingly antagonistic ideas?

> But Christ is faithful over God's house as a son. And we are his house, if indeed we hold fast our confidence and our boasting in our hope.
> (Hebrews 3:6)

> Since then we have a great high priest who has passed through the heavens, Jesus, the Son of God, let us hold fast our confession.
> (Hebrews 4:14)

> So that by two unchangeable things, in which it is impossible for God to lie, we who have fled for refuge might have strong encouragement to hold fast to the hope set before us.
> (Hebrews 6:18)

> Let us hold fast the confession of our hope without wavering, for he who promised is faithful.
> (Hebrews 10:23)

Hold On, Can't Lose

There seems to be no question the Hebrew writer is talking to genuine Christians. His language in Hebrews 10:26–39 points to the prior redemptive work of God on behalf of his audience (Philippians 1:6). Not only does the writer lump himself in the group of people who could walk away from the faith, but he uses salvific and robust language to talk about God's past regenerative work in their lives

(Romans 8:29-30). He is not leaning into vague or arbitrary "profession language." His words communicate possession language. Check out these verses.

- **VERSE 26:** If we go on sinning. (Note the pronoun we—he includes himself with them.)
- **VERSE 26:** They have received the knowledge of the truth.
- **VERSE 29:** They were sanctified.
- **VERSE 32:** They were enlightened.

The author of Hebrews is doing what he wants them to do for each other—bring stern warnings regarding the danger of choosing sin while walking away from Christ (Hebrews 10:24-25). The kind of writing he is using is the kind of communication I would use for myself or any other born again (John 3:7) follower of Christ. How different is his language from what you might use if you talked to a friend who was considering walking away from the faith or living in objective sin?

Dangerous Believers

> For if we go on sinning deliberately after receiving the knowledge of the truth, there no longer remains a sacrifice for sins.
> (Hebrews 10:26)

> It is a fearful thing to fall into the hands of the living God.
> (Hebrews 10:31)

> But my righteous one shall live by faith, and if he shrinks back, my soul has no pleasure in him. But we are not of those who shrink back and are destroyed, but of those who have faith and preserve their souls.
> (Hebrews 10:38-39)

We all know how Christians experience salvation by grace through faith in the works of Jesus Christ. To have justification (Romans 8:29–30), we exercise faith, not works, as seen in many passages throughout the New Testament, e.g., Romans 1:17; Ephesians 1:3-14, 2:8-9; Titus 3:5. Salvation is not loseable. We all know this. But the writer of Hebrews is bringing a strong warning to those God sanctified, enlightened, and gave the knowledge of the truth, and he includes himself in the number of those who need to be warned (Hebrews 10:26). He does not say God condemns us, as though we would go to hell for walking away from God, but he is clear: the Lord is not pleased when we mock His gospel. He is not happy about people who continue in willful sin.

Perilous Presumption

> God disciplines His children harshly when they continue in willful defiance. And He does so in one of two ways. Either He takes their lives, or He judicially sentences them to live out their lives experiencing the consequences of their sin.
> —Chuck Swindoll

The writer is making a strong appeal, hoping they will know how this stubborn refusal to walk away from sin will cause God's anger to come down on them. Walking away from God tramples the Son of God underfoot. It is an insult to the Spirit of grace who enlightened us to see the Son in the first place. It would be a travesty, insult, and mockery to show no gratitude, humility, or obedient response to the One who gave His life to save us. How can we say there is more life in our sin than in Christ alone? This concept is why I appealed to my counselee, who was more in love with his sin than his Savior.

There is no place in the Bible where it means there is

grace for the consequences of sin. There will be severe consequences for a defiant believer. Insulting the Spirit of grace, who is trying to draw you back, but you do not care and refuse to walk away from your sin, is to trample underfoot the grace of God that can save you from the consequences of your stubbornness. My friend was in a dangerous place. He came to counseling buzzed, flippant, snarky, sarcastic, and comical about the counseling. His wife was crying, and my soul was sad for them.

Gospel Abuse

I am not ready to say that he was unsaved. I did not feel that God or His gospel needed theological protection by me causally categorizing him as having made a profession but not indeed possessing Jesus. This kind of thinking could be a gospel travesty. Maybe there are more than two Christian types: those who authentically believe in Jesus and never walk away, or those who say they believe in Jesus and can walk away. Christianity is not that neat, and sin has never been that respectful. The Hebrew writer is saying there is a third Christian type—a believer who, for whatever reasons, spurns the grace he once received. The writer did not want to dilute the gospel by protecting it from the possibility of this kind of abuse. To not embrace this third type of Christian is to presume against God's grace (Psalm 19:13). You and I experience temptation every day. We are under pressure while suffering the ebb and flow of victory and defeat throughout our lives. It may keep our Christianity and our theology in tight and neat packages, but it can be a massive disservice to the body of Christ.

No one is exempt from the cursedness of life, whether the curse comes from our hearts or the world we live in— even the believer's heart. At the time of the writing of the book of Hebrews, the believers were under persecution. They believed in Christ by faith and maybe even enjoyed a refreshing time through Christ and their community. In time, the cares and troubles of life began to mount, and some of them decided to walk away from Christ. It would have been easy to say they were never Christians, but it would not have served them or the community to quickly determine if they were in the faith. The Hebrew writer was not going to categorize them willy-nilly as false converts.

Call to Action

Can you see how dangerous it is not to warn a person of the consequences of walking away from God? The ones who walked away would not have received the warning of the impending danger of spurning their faith. Those still persevering needed to know the risks of this kind of thinking and living. To wipe your hands of them does not help them or those who may yet choose sin over Christ. The Hebrew writer would not check the theological box of "God never saved them in the first place" and move on to the next thing. His heart was broken, which is why his language was so severe. He gave us a threefold call to action regarding our friends. His first point was to consider those in our immediate community of faith. You see this in the passage—Hebrews 10:19-39: consider, confront, and comfort.

Consider

> And let us consider how to stir up one another to love and good works, not neglecting to meet together, as is the habit of some, but encouraging one another.
> (Hebrews 10:24-25)

- How much time do you spend during your day considering those you can impact with the gospel?
- Do your friends feel "considered" by you?

There is no question these Hebrew believers felt considered by the writer of this book. He could not have been more clear. He understood them, their history, their lifestyles, and their temptations. He did not hold back from giving them careful consideration while laying out a clear plan to keep persevering in the faith God had granted them. It would be a joy to be in the Hebrew writer's small group! One of the big disappointments in today's church is how brothers and sisters will not give up the time needed to consider how to stir up each other to love and do good deeds.

Confront

For if we go on sinning deliberately after receiving the knowledge of the truth, there no longer remains a sacrifice for sins, but a fearful expectation of judgment and a fury of fire that will consume the adversaries.

(Hebrews 10:26–27)

- Have your friends experienced your carefully considered corrective care?
- Do your friends clearly understand the consequences of their actions because you have warned them?

There is no place for harshness within the Christian community. If you want to know how to warn without being mean-spirited about it, carefully read this passage. You feel the writer's affection for the people. He says some of the sternest and most direct things you can speak to a person, but you do not feel talked down to or verbally assaulted. He loved those people enough to warn them about the possibilities of their actions. He was like a father to them. Any good father would warn a son or daughter about the dangers in our world and the consequences of choosing those risks (Luke 11:11).

Comfort

> But recall the former days when, after you were enlightened, you endured a hard struggle with sufferings, sometimes being publicly exposed to reproach and affliction, and sometimes being partners with those so treated.
>
> (Hebrews 10:32–33)

The Hebrew writer was not like a hit-and-run driver. He was with them, willing to stick it out for their good and God's glory. He confronted and comforted. He reminded them of the efficacious grace of God that was evident in their lives. He wanted them to know how God will be with them in the future by reminding them how He was with them in the past. He identified evidence of God's gracious activity in their lives.

- When you consider and confront your friends, do they also experience your comfort?
- Would you be categorized more as a critical corrector or a comforting confronter?

A Christian can turn his nose to God and walk away from the faith. That does not mean he has a broken relationship with God, though he may sever his fellowship (1 John 1:7–10) with God and others. It also means there will be consequences for taking God's grace for granted (Galatians 6:7–10). May we all be warned. May we all respond by graciously seeking to change ourselves while carefully considering others within our faith communities.

> If you are left without discipline, in which all have participated, then you are illegitimate children and not sons.
>
> (Hebrews 12:8)

It is a fearful thing to fall into the hands of the living God.
(Hebrews 10:31)

3

Steps to a Hard Heart

It is possible to know God but still have a hard heart. Though we have many means of grace, like prayer, the Bible, our local churches, and each other, Christians are not impervious to the infiltration of sin or its dastardly effects. It only takes a little evil to create havoc in our souls. Knowing and experiencing God does not prevent us from moving down the path to hard-heartedness, making it critical to understand how to diagnose the sequence that leads to a hard heart.

Can God?

May I ask: How has your week been? Has the resurrected Lord stabilized your thoughts as you have reflected on our victory through Him? How has the residual effect of Christ's coming out of the tomb affected your life this week? The resurrection was a singular event intended to have continuous power. It's like a recyclable gift you can use over and over again. It never loses its influence or impact in the Christian's life. It never diminishes from what it can do for us, even if we have been Christians for decades. The conquering power of the Lord that secures our victory should sustain all of His children through every day and every event of our lives. There is no diminishing of the joy, hope, and power we experienced when we first heard about Christ's salvation, as it buoys us through all trials or challenges (2 Corinthians 1:8-9). However, we live in the real world, which is a fallen one. The temptation to give up and even question God's active goodness on our behalf happens, especially during seasons of disappointment. Listen to how the Hebrews questioned God during their wilderness wandering.

> He made streams come out of the rock and caused waters to flow down like rivers. Yet they sinned still more against him, rebelling against the Most High in the desert. They tested God in their heart by demanding the food they craved. They spoke against God, saying, "Can God spread a table in the wilderness?"
>
> (Psalm 78:16-19)

In Exodus 17:1-7, just three itty bitty chapters from God's great victory of leading the children of Israel through the Red Sea, His children were bitterly complaining about their new and disappointing circumstances. They were thirsty and wanted water. Imagine that! I can't believe those people! They experienced God in all His profoundness. They saw Him do the spectacular, which was beyond anyone's comprehension. They were the choicest recipients of His miracle working power. Almighty God poured unmitigated blessings on them.

God Can

What they did would be analogous to us leaving our local church meetings on Easter Sunday and beginning to complain and grumble before exiting the parking lot. A critical spirit is the perfect illustration of what the small-minded Israelites were doing. Though the miracle of the resurrection should be enough to equip any Christian through any trial that may come upon them, it can become just another lifeless past event with no current sustaining power. Present testing should be the motivation to reflect on God's past faithfulness to stabilize us through our trials. The backward reflection on God's past demonstration is the antidote to trust Him through present difficulties. The children of Israel were complaining and whining right after seeing one of the most miraculous events in the Bible. How many days after Sunday's worship service do you feel more like Pharaoh and his army crushed by the encompassing waters of the Red Sea rather than the Israelites who walked through it?

The question the Israelites needed to wrestle with was whether God's provision through the exodus was enough for them to rest in His ongoing care. We have a similar question we need to wrestle with too. Is the Lord's one-time gospel work that earned our salvation enough to satisfy us while giving us hope and direction when our circumstances are not as expected? The Israelites went off the rails quickly. Their problems became greater than God's victory. Being problem-centered rather than God-centered led to grumbling and complaining, which is a bold accusation against the active goodness of God in their lives. They should have reflected on God's past care and moved forward in faith, knowing God would come through for them again, again, and again. What more could the Lord have done for them than to show His faithfulness to them? He already divided the sea so they could be born again. How much are we like those unbelieving believers?

Be Warned

The critical moments in our lives are when we perceive insurmountable odds and unremitting difficulties. These are the times when we should focus our hearts on God's past ability to triumph despite the odds that appear to be against us. Humanity was born to worship, which should come with a large caution flag: we can quickly shift from worshiping our Deliverer to worshiping our self-reliant means to extricate ourselves from our troubles. Because the Israelites were not getting what they wanted, they chose to walk away from the Lord. Their hearts hardened because of unmet expectations. If we walk away from the Lord, what hope do we have? Our real hope is in Jesus and Him alone. There is a warning for us through the story of the Israelites not to let discouraging circumstances harden our hearts.

> Therefore, as the Holy Spirit says, "Today, if you hear his voice, do not harden your hearts as in the rebellion, on the day of testing in the wilderness, where your fathers put me to the test and saw my works for forty years."
>
> (Hebrews 3:7–10)

If God saved His people through the exodus and, despite this, their hearts became hard when life became hard, be warned: we can harden our hearts like them if we don't heed the caution. We are no different from the Israelites in the wilderness. What they fell prey to is our temptation as well. We will easily and quickly develop a hard heart if we don't remind ourselves of the gospel—the exodus Christ provided for us through His death, resurrection, and ascension. A hard heart is the Hebrew writer's main point in this section to his believing audience. He knew a true believer could drift from the gospel to the point where his salvation did not impact his sanctification.

Functional Atheism

> Take care, brothers, lest there be in any of you an evil, unbelieving heart, leading you to fall away from the living God. But exhort one another every day, as long as it is called "today," that none of you may be hardened by the deceitfulness of sin. For we share in Christ, if indeed we hold our original confidence firm to the end.
>
> (Hebrews 3:12–14)

These strong warnings in Hebrews are not saying we can lose our salvation or that God never saved us; they are saying that we can lose the resurrection power that our salvation offers us. God can save us, and we can be on our way to heaven but lost in the temporal circumstances of our lives. We can have eternal life but lose our way in the here and now to where the reality of our problems overwhelms our salvation. There is only one answer to this kind of problem. It's the gospel, powerfully displayed through the resurrection of Christ. If the gospel is insufficient for our present trials, we will be susceptible to a hard heart.

Just like the Israelites in the Old Testament who lost sight of God's power displayed at the Red Sea, we can lose sight of the empty tomb to the point where our disappointment becomes an accusation toward God. The core issue in this passage is an ongoing, undiagnosed, untreated heart condition. The warning is to assess ourselves soberly so that we don't have an evil and unbelieving heart. The hardening of the believer's heart will result in functional atheism or what I call an *unbelieving believer* (Mark 9:24). The Christian living in functional atheism is looking for deliverance from present circumstances rather than trusting in God's prior deliverance through the gospel. The Lord will not give us complete victory in our current circumstances. His desire is not so much about giving us everything we want but for us to trust Him at all times.

Hardening Process

The Israelites forgot about God's past power while demanding He meets their present disappointment according to their expectations. Do not be naive. Unbiblical expectations can happen to any of us. The Hebrew writer warned the readers by reminding them of what happened to their ancestors. Since the Hebrew letter's writing, millions of Christians have drifted from their faith. They hardened their hearts. They enthusiastically went into their new salvation, and life slapped them in the face. Someone hurt their feelings; they had crushed dreams and dashed hopes. The disappointment began to make its appeal in their hearts. The hardening process was so imperceptible that they did not discern it until they became case-hardened. You do not want this to happen to you. But it can. None of us are bulletproof. No matter how we may want to think about ourselves, we're just one disappointment from walking away from the Lord. Developing a hard heart happens in four contiguous steps: evil, unbelief, drifting, and hardness. Let's take a quick look at all four of these steps.

1. **EVIL:** God allows evil into our lives. From a biblical perspective, that is normal and expected (Genesis 50:20). We live in a sinful world. Fallen people are all around us, and so are we. Evil was also a promise from the Lord (Genesis 3:18). The real problem is not so much the evil but a lack of understanding of the purposes of the evil in our lives.
2. **UNBELIEF:** The regression to a hard heart begins when the person who experiences evil questions God's active goodness in his life. Two of the most

common ways this "kind of unbelief" happens are through grumbling and complaining. Both of these are manifestations of anger. The complainer is missing the Lord in his mess while demanding God meet his expectations according to his desires. This first false step opens him up to more sin. The genuinely believing heart begins a slow and almost unseeable process of no longer believing in God. His friends, including Christians, often do not discern his unbelief—not until it's too late.

3. **DRIFTING:** If the grumbling persists, the person will begin to take steps away from God. The Bible will become cold to him. He will start to move away from the people of God. His prayer closet will become silent.

4. **HARDNESS:** Grumbling and complaining are two ways of pointing the finger at God while expressing disappointment in Him for not coming through for us. It says, "I'm right in this matter, and You are wrong, and You need to subscribe to my solutions." Over time this will become a habit, and the conscience will harden to the point where the person can no longer perceive what he is doing to himself. There will be an insensitivity to and detachment from the Spirit's voice as well as the voices of his friends.

Ounce of Prevention

FIRST PREVENTATIVE: Don't be naive. The Hebrew writer is also giving us a strong warning. The Lord thought enough about this to put it in His forever Word. Hardness can happen to me. It can happen to you. Your first call to action regarding this caution is to humbly ask the Lord if any wicked way is working in your heart (Psalm 139:23). If you have not already perceived your vulnerability to a hard heart as you reflect on these things, maybe the hardening process has already begun. If your first thoughts have been about someone else, be warned: the process may have already started in your heart.

Second preventative: You are vulnerable. Just as our bodies are susceptible to different germ intruders, your soul is always in the crosshairs of the satanic ones (1 Peter 5:8). They would find no greater pleasure than to take you down, and it's easier than most of us imagine. Preach the gospel to yourself every day, throughout your day. The gospel is the antidote for a hard heart. If you're not daily marinating your mind in the victory the Lord wrought for you, His victory will become powerless in your present circumstances.

Third preventative: Love your friends. Your friends are just like you. We're all naive and vulnerable. We're no match for the devil and his schemes. If our hearts are not riveted to God's provision—as experienced by the gospel—we're easy-picking for the evil one. You must, moment by moment, fortify your heart with gospel goodness. And as you do, you must have a courageous and grace-filled boldness to speak to your fellow brothers and sisters who are also easily tempted to jump on the path to a hard heart.

Call to Action

The Hebrew writer was warning his friends. He knew the dangers. The Old Testament is a clear testimony of people who did not know how to steward their disappointments. In three short chapters from their Red Sea experience, they were already accusing God, ready to return to their former lifestyles. You must be appropriately heeding the warning about the dangers of a hard heart. Perhaps these questions will help you assess your heart and make any necessary recalibrations.

1. How has the residual effect of Christ's coming out of the tomb affected your life this week?
2. How are you situating your thoughts in your victory in the resurrected Jesus?
3. Are you actively engaging your friends in a comparable way the Hebrew writer was engaging that community?
4. Who engages you this way? Do you have that kind of friend? If not, how will you build this kind of intrusive relationship?
5. What changes do you need to make to your life or community as a preventative measure to keep from a hard heart?

Steps to a Hard Heart

4

When I Was Silent

Are you more concerned about what God thinks about your sin or what others think about your sin? How you answer this question will determine the quality of your life and the way you interact with your friends. If you're more concerned about God's view of you, there will be a desire to live openly and honestly before Him and others. However, if the opinions of others have more control over you, the temptation to hide your true self while presenting a false narrative will be immense. To know what has more power is by assessing your willingness to be appropriately transparent with your friends.

When I Kept Silent

I'm not suggesting that you broadly share your sins, faults, or mistakes to anyone. I'm speaking of your willingness (or unwillingness) to share your life and relationships with an appropriate person. Whether you share your life with others depends on several things, but your desire to do so reveals your motivation and what has the most control over you. Suppose God's opinion of you has the most control over your life. In that case, you have your answer: you are a humble, God-centered, God-glorifying, sin-mortifying, Christlike example more concerned with Christ's reputation than your own. But if you are more concerned with what others think, to the point that you are motivated to hide your sin, you are in more trouble than you could ever imagine. Listen to David.

> For when I kept silent, my bones wasted away through my groaning all day long. For day and night your hand was heavy upon me; my strength was dried up as by the heat of summer.
> (Psalm 32:3-4)

King David lived in both extremes. After he had committed adultery, he began to cover his tracks for about a year. Because he was not willing to come clean regarding his sin, the Lord did for him what he was not going to do for himself. The merciful Lord sent Nathan to break his heart and expose his deception. Before Nathan's visit, David commented on what his life was like when he tried to bury the sin he committed. If this is you, study Psalm 32:3-4 carefully. If this passage does not put the fear of God in you, perhaps you are in deeper weeds than you realize. David lied and connived for nearly twelve months, pretending all was well when all was unwell. He was trying to ignore what he did, though he could not hide his sin from the One who could see into the dark. There is only one way to escape from what had captured his heart: walking through the door of humility, confession, honesty, and transparency. You and I can fake out each other, but we cannot deceive the Lord. Even if we could keep the illusion going for a season, there would eventually be a payday someday. The longer we resist the truth by holding on to lies, the more complicated our lives and relationships will become.

> And no creature is hidden from his sight, but all are naked and exposed to the eyes of him to whom we must give account.
> (Hebrews 4:13)

Pushing Truth Aside

> *For the wrath of God is revealed from heaven against all ungodliness and unrighteousness of men, who by their unrighteousness suppress the truth.*
>
> (Romans 1:18)

Paul gives more insight into what David was experiencing when he laid out the degenerating process to the Romans of what happens when a person attempts to press the truth of God out of their lives. He talked about how God's wrath—His angry displeasure—would rain down from heaven on anyone who lived in ungodly and unrighteous ways. Paul said this happened when people volitionally chose to press the truth of God from their lives. To suppress the truth is to squeeze it out of our lives. It is like pushing down on a balloon filled with water: the water shifts to the right and the left. It distorts what was once balanced. When we press the truth of God from our lives by holding on to or propagating deception, we will have distorted souls. We cannot exchange the truth of God for a lie while worshipping the creature more than the Creator and expect distortion not to happen in some way (Romans 1:25). David did this though he knew the truth about God. He was a man after the Lord's heart (1 Samuel 13:14), but he chose a path of sin. The sadness is not so much about the kind of immorality (adultery) that he picked, which is bad enough, but the deception he propagated after his transgression—a process that began to break down his body and soul. How could it be any other way?

Dulling the Inner Voice

> *Today, if you hear his voice, do not harden your hearts.*
>
> (Hebrews 4:7)

In Hebrews, we learn more about how ongoing and unrepented sin dulls our inner being. Do you understand the downward progression of someone who refuses to deal rightly with sin? While the physical debilitation that David went through was horrible enough, the dulling of his conscience may have been the worst of all. The conscience (Latin: co-knowledge) is our inner voice. The conscience is the moral thermostat that tells us when we are doing what is right or wrong. Suppose your inner voice becomes dull of hearing (Hebrews 5:11). In that case, you are unhooking yourself from God's morality while choosing a path that appears to be wise from your vantage point (Isaiah 5:21). Paul said people like this were not wise but fools (Romans 1:22). Uncoupling oneself from God's morality with no moral compass releases the individual to be a god of his life (Proverbs 14:12).

The worst case of this is Lucifer. Though no one will do what he did, there are no known limits to what a depraved soul can do without God's restrictions. Sometimes people ask, "Can you believe what [he] did?" Almost without exception, I say, "I can believe it if [he] has been living apart from God in a self-absorbed way. I am surprised you are surprised by their actions." Paul talked about this perspective to his young protégé, Timothy, as he was teaching him what could happen when deceitfulness and insincerity were in play. He said people participating in such things would sear their consciences (1 Timothy 4:2). A seared *co-knowledge* is equivalent to the cattleman placing an orange-hot iron brand on the cow's rump to the point of searing its hide. The seared spot does not have any sensation. Callousness is a dangerous thing when it happens to a person's conscience. David was heading that way. He was willfully exchanging the truth of God for a lie, and he was not about to alter his course. Fortunately, someone loved him enough to do for him what he was not going to do for himself.

Enter Nathan.

Turn on the Light

> Nathan said to David, "You are the man..."
>
> (2 SaFmuel 12:7)

The Lord nudged Nathan to go to his friend. You know the story. One of the fantastic things about this story is that David did not get the point of Nathan's fictitious monologue (2 Samuel 12:1-6). Nathan was talking, and David was not hearing (Matthew 11:15). He was so dim-sighted, detached, dull, and determined to hide his sin that he did not have ears to hear or eyes to see. Nathan stopped beating around the sheep gate with his sheep story and spoke plainly to David. Never underestimate the hardening process of the conscience when a person refuses to own their sin. Do not expect them to see what is right in front of them. It is as plain as the nose on your face because you are walking in the light. Light does that to a person. Any person, including Christians, can walk in darkness. John reminded believers of this truth when discussing how sin can complicate the Christian's life.

> But if we walk in the light, as he is in the light, we have fellowship with one another, and the blood of Jesus his Son cleanses us from all sin. If we say we have no sin, we deceive ourselves, and the truth is not in us.
>
> (1 John 1:7-8)

David was saying, "I have no sin." If John were there, he would respond, "You have deceived yourself, and the truth is not in you." That is why David could not understand what Nathan was trying to accomplish. If we are sitting around waiting for a person—who is willfully pressing the truth of God out of their lives—to come clean, we may not only be sitting around for a long time, but we may be culpable. We could be enabling them in their sin because we did not speak the truth to them—the Word they could not see. After all, they turned off the light in their souls. Do not underestimate the power of sin. Do not underestimate what it can do to a person's conscience. Do not think you have no moral responsibility to bring the light to them so they can see. I'm not suggesting their sin is your fault, but Christianity is not a spectator sport. God expects us to be active, secondary agents in each other's lives.

Hurt Your Friend

> Faithful are the wounds of a friend; profuse are the kisses of an enemy.
>
> (Proverbs 27:6)

Wounding David is the kindest thing Nathan could do for his friend. Saying hard things reminds me of my favorite quote from my former professor, Wayne Mack. When thinking about doing hard things to someone, he said, "You can hate me now and love me later, or you can love me now and hate me later." I doubt David ever hated Nathan for what he did, but there is no question that Nathan brought pain into David's life. Nathan loved him so much that he had no choice but to hurt his friend. If you logically follow David's downward progression in Psalm 32:3–4, there seems to be little question that David was deteriorating physically and spiritually by the day.

David's confession in that Psalm reads like he would not have lived much longer. Things went wrong quickly for David. God's mercy imposed itself on David's life by sending someone to wound him. He reacted blindly, impulsively, and wrongly to Nathan's sheep story. When he discovered he was the story's leading actor, he shut his mouth, started listening, and later responded appropriately (Job 40:4–5). Without interruption, he let his friend speak. The fantastic news is that the Spirit quickened his hard heart once his eyes were open, and he knew immediately what he did and how to respond. When Nathan finished, David said the only thing that needed to be said, "I have sinned against the LORD" (2 Samuel 12:13). Six words summed it up.

Will You Choose Life?

There was nothing else to say because nothing else mattered at that moment. David sinned against more people than the Lord, but only one thing mattered at that crucial time. This point brings us to my opening statement: "Are you more concerned about what God thinks about your sin or what others think about your sin? How you answer this question will determine the quality of your life and the way you interact with your friends." After David had sinned, he plotted a deceptive plan to cover up his actions. He hurt many people in the process. The only thing that mattered was for others not to know what he did. It was a bold move for someone after the Lord's heart.

How could someone be so connected to God and be so self-deceived? David's life is a call for us to do reflective self-examination. If someone who loved God so much could fall so far, how much more possible is it for you or me to detach our hearts from the truth we know? While his adultery was horrendous and his deception was causing physical and spiritual suicide, the fantastic thing about this story is his restoration. Like the prodigal son, the only thing that mattered to him was restoration (Luke 15:17–22). You can discern a person's sincerity by the radicalness of their repentance. The prodigal son threw in the white towel and gave up all control of his life to his father. David did similarly.

I am not suggesting you broadcast your sin to the world, but I am suggesting you be willing to do anything necessary to restore what sin destroyed. In David's case, you see how he walked out his repentance. He broadcasted it to the world: Psalm 32:1-11 and Psalm 51:1-19. The most effective way for us to test the genuineness of our repentance is by giving up control of the situation to those we trust and who have proven themselves faithful to the practical applications of God's Word in our lives. If our repentance is more about controlling the outcomes, we are not in a repenting frame of mind. But if we are willing to give up control of our lives and situations by humbly submitting to those who can help us, we should expect God's fantastic favor (James 4:6).

Call to Action

1. How silent are you about your sin?
2. If you are afraid to share your struggles, why are you?
3. What are you trying to protect? What are you trying to control? What are you trying to hide?
4. Are you willing to bury your actions and reap the consequences, regardless of what they are? If so, why?
5. What if you listen to Nathan and respond like David? If you are willing, will you talk to someone today?

Blessed is the one whose transgression is forgiven, whose sin is covered. Blessed is the man against whom the Lord counts no iniquity, and in whose spirit there is no deceit.

(Psalm 32:1-2)

5

My Friend's Sin Secret

Your friend comes to you with a secret sin. You are his accountability partner, and he asks you to keep his sin secret. How would you respond to him? Is it okay to pledge confidentiality or have an expectation of it? Does confidentiality have value in the context of confession, or does it interfere with the benefits of confession? Are there instances where we should tell others about a transgression, even if the guilty party is against it? What biblical principles should guide us regarding sin, secret keeping, and sharing inside of a biblical community?

Applying Words

Though there are several questions to work through, let's begin with the word confidentiality. First, it is not a Bible word, not making it wrong or inappropriate but ensuring we have a biblical framework and worldview when discussing communication puzzles. Christians have brought this modern construction from secular counseling into the application of presumed biblical communication principles. Words are important. Our Christian faith and practice stand or fall on how we think about and apply words (John 17:17; 2 Timothy 3:16–17). Word selection and use require our utmost care. For example, theologians have stood at the door of the Word of God for centuries, protecting against any misuse of God's Word while helping us to understand it correctly. They knew the only way we could have faith in God was by His Word (Romans 10:17).

Historical theologians have lived and died protecting God's Word from theological error (2 Timothy 4:6-7). The call for theological vigilance and precision has always been paramount for the Christian. One of the odd developments in the past century is how the Christian community has not been as vigilant regarding our *sanctification words*. While we can be exacting in parsing the Greek, which we should be meticulous in doing, we can be sloppy when thinking about and developing sanctification processes. Sound theology is merely an excellent beginning to a God-glorifying life. Sound sanctification is just as necessary as good theology because sanctification is the assumed outflow of our theological understanding.

A succinct definition of sanctification is the application of theology. Theological knowledge without biblical application can make one arrogant (1 Corinthians 8:1). It's isolated head knowledge. Biblical application without sound theology can make one foolish. (See the "fool verses" in Proverbs.) Wisdom happens when Christians couple sound theological information with practical applications in real-world relationships and contexts (2 Timothy 3:16-17). The call of God is not only to be a stickler about theology but to be just as picky about how we apply our theology. There is a blindside to our sanctification that we must guard just as fiercely as our theological prowess. If we are not as exacting in how we think about sanctification, we're on the road to being a devil—someone familiar with the Bible but who does not accurately apply it (Genesis 3:1; James 2:19).

Being Confidential

Because the Bible has a more thorough way of discussing confidentiality in the broader framework of communication, you could extract the word confidential from our Christian vocabulary without compromising what some folks are attempting to solve. Confidentiality is the world's approach to problem-solving, not the Bible's. Christians should not think this way because the Bible provides a better way to think about communication. Let me make this point by telling you a story.

Biff was his pastor's accountability partner. As time passed, Biff learned that his pastor struggled with a porn addiction, a thirty-year secret. Eventually, the church terminated the pastor for other reasons, though those character-related problems contributed to his porn problem. The elders knew about the character deficiencies but did not know the breadth and depth of his problems. Within a few weeks, the recently fired pastor began looking for another ministry job. Biff appealed to him to come clean with the churches interviewing him. The unemployed pastor refused while holding Biff to the secularized standard of confidentiality.

Paul gave the Corinthian church a public rebuke for keeping silent about sexual sin (1 Corinthians 5:12). King David talked about how awful it was to stay quiet about his sin (Psalm 32:3-4), and God sent Nathan to confront David (2 Samuel 12:7). Paul warned the Corinthians about how their lack of appropriate confrontation leads to even greater public scrutiny and judgment (1 Corinthians 6:1). When sinful offenses happen, our first call to action should be redemptive measures, not secretive ones. Overlooking this point about sin is similar to cancer: it will continue to spread, rolling over and affecting more people (1 Corinthians 5:6).

Better Words

Though the Bible does not discuss confidentiality, it is not silent on the matter. God's Word has much to say about how to talk about our relational problems—after you reframe the language biblically. Confidentiality fits under the communication umbrella, teaching us how we should communicate with each other, especially on sensitive matters. The word communication comes from the word community or the Greek word koinonia. The word koinonia means fellowship, community, or participation, which indicates how we are to interrelate with each other in the body of Christ. The primary way we have relational interaction with each other is through how we communicate with each other.

- Koinonia is moving toward unity, transparency, honesty, integrity, vulnerability, trust, and redemption.
- Confidentiality moves toward secrets, hiding, fear, distrust, and even deception in some situations.

Confidentiality does not have biblical moorings, which can lead to sub- and unbiblical applications. The story of Biff and his former pastor illustrates how this can be a problem. The Bible gives better words that teach us how to build community through communication without harming others. Here are a few examples. As you reflect on these words, let the Bible impress you as it teaches how to govern our tongues while broadening God's assumptions for critical conversations.

Discretion	Building up	Fitting speech
Backbiting	Unwholesome	Soft answer
Judicious	Confession	Ungodly speech
Slander	Slow to speak	Rash words
Gambling	Wise words	Gossip

Of course, there are many more words about communication in the Bible that encourage or convict us about how we talk to and about each other. Here are a few verses, not to mention all of James 3:1-18. See 1 Peter 3:1-9; Ephesians 4:15, 4:25, and 5:22-33; James 1:19; Proverbs 10:29, 12:18, 13:17, 15:1-2, 16:23, 17:27, and 25:11-15; James 1:5; and Matthew 12:37.

Biblical Restoration

In the case of the secretive pastor, he likes the word confidentiality because he wants to hide his sin from view. Matthew provides a governing passage for how we should think about this pastor while never deviating from other directives regarding our tongues. Remember, the goal is not confidentiality but community and restoration, which will happen in proportion to us being built up in the unity of the faith (Ephesians 4:13-16). The community question, as opposed to the confidentiality question, should motivate us to ask, "How can we have a better community within the body of Christ, rather than how can we seek to keep our sinful secrets confidential?" A biblical community has proper motivation for unity while a fearful one typically prefers confidentiality, desiring to keep secrets.

> If your brother sins against you, go and tell him his fault, between you and him alone. If he listens to

you, you have gained your brother. But if he does not listen, take one or two others along with you, that every charge may be established by the evidence of two or three witnesses. If he refuses to listen to them, tell it to the church. And if he refuses to listen even to the church, let him be to you as a Gentile and a tax collector.
(Matthew 18:15–17)

The humble, gospelized person has nothing to hide or fear and constantly pushes toward greater integration within Christ's body. Christ came to give us a biblical community (koinonia). He has always desired to reverse the curse that includes bringing light to covert operations (Romans 8:1). Adam put on fig leaves to cover his fear, guilt, and shame because he was more interested in secret keeping than open, honest care and accountability (Genesis 3:7–10). We do not want to mimic Adam (Ephesians 5:11). We want to follow Christ (1 Corinthians 11:1). We do this through confession, which is agreeing with God about the actual condition of ourselves while walking out repentance within a community of appropriate friends (1 John 1:7–10). The people who do this will experience biblical koinonia in the body of Christ.

Loving Brothers

There will be times when a Christian sins. There is a process for restoring him to God. The first step is his confession. If the person confesses his sin to God, he can receive instant forgiveness while stepping on the path to freedom from his sin. But if sin has caught him and he cannot or will not extricate himself (like the pastor), he will need external restoration from those within the community (Galatians 6:1–2). This opportunity is where Matthew 18:15–17 releases us from secular worldviews about how to help people change.

If a person is not willing to clean up his act or cannot clean up his act, the Lord calls the body of Christ to engage the erring friend for His glory, the person's benefit, the body's health, and a warning to all.

These reasons are why I would never pledge to keep things confidential with anyone. If someone were to appeal to me to keep what they are about to say confidential, I would tell them that I can't make that pledge because I do not know what they will say to me. What if they told me about sexually abusing an underage child? It does not mean I am to gossip about or slander them. The opposite of extracting confidentiality from our language is not permission to gossip or slander anyone. Scripture commands that we should not let an erring believer continue in sin. There is a beautiful biblical symmetry between communication that honors discretion and dialogue that celebrates redemptive work in a person's life, which is the entire point of Matthew 18:15-17.

The process for Biff should have been to let his pastor friend know that he would talk to the elder board to get him biblical help if he was unwilling to take this initiative. He had already made many appeals for him to change. Sin had captured the pastor, a problem that eventually cost him his church, though more importantly, it was a besmirching of God's name, hurting the body of Christ, and could—possibly—endanger innocent people. The Lord executed His Son because of our transgressions (Isaiah 53:10)—a clue that informs us how seriously God takes our sin. For us to hide our problems from others is to mock the death of Christ. The issue is not about slander or gossip but about responding appropriately redemptive on behalf of a person who refuses to act redemptively for himself.

Case Study Application

If a friend is in sin and the community of faith does not act upon what they know, the community of faith becomes guilty to some degree. Think about it this way: would you want a secret porn addict pastoring your children? Would you hire a porn addict to lead and shepherd your church? Of course, not. What if we take my questions in the beginning and push them through the filter of community and communication rather than through the filter of confidentiality?

- *How would you respond to Biff?* When I'm an accountability partner with someone who has secret sins, I need grace-filled courage to let him know I will do everything within my biblical rights to motivate him to be honest with God and others, even if it means letting others know about his problem should he refuse to repent.
- *Is it okay to pledge confidentiality or have an expectation of it?* I will let my friend know that I will love him to the end. I will also let him know I will use the utmost discretion and stewardship regarding what he tells me. He will know that my love for him may mean I will make some hard decisions if he continues to choose a life of unrepentant sin. I cannot hide his sin because I love him too much.
- *Does confidentiality have value in the context of confession?* Discretion has value. Wisdom has value. We should never tolerate slander and gossip. Therefore, I will guard my tongue when he confesses sin to me, but because I love him, I cannot keep his issues secret if he chooses not to repent. He will not hold me to an unbiblical standard if he genuinely loves me. He will want me to get all the appropriate help necessary so that he can be free.

- *Are there instances where we should tell others about a transgression, even if the guilty party is against it?* I have no choice but to ask others to become involved with my friend who refuses to repent. Not to do so would be like watching a friend bleed to death in front of me while not acting on it. Biblical love must override biblical hate. Matthew 18:15–17 is my guide. 1 Corinthians 6:1 is my warning. If I do not do this for him, the sin he wants me to hide may become more public than he ever imagined.
- *What biblical principles guide us in this?* There is no one principle to guide, but there is a gospel to emulate. The gospel is about redeeming, restoring, rescuing, and rejoicing. I want to follow my Lord by being redemptive in the lives of my brothers and sisters in Christ. Though I hope to never sin against any of them with my words, I am bound to use my words in the fullest redemptive means possible, even if it causes relational conflict within the community of faith.

Call to Action

1. What are some instances where you would not share a person's sin?
2. What are a couple of other instances where you have no choice but to let others know?
3. Why is it wise never to promise confidentiality before someone shares something with you?
4. Will you review the biblical words and terms I gave in the table and talk about how the Bible's view of communication is better than the purposes of confidentiality while not making the "confidential mistake" that the pastor made?

6

Reasons for No Change

Every person who comes to you does not always fully invest themselves in being free from their problems. I'm not suggesting that they are insincere. I'm speaking to the complexity of some issues and the accompanying heart entanglements that have become part of a person's life for so long that the habituation's strength is more powerful than the motivation to change. Just because they share their trouble with you does not mean they will put in the effort to change or know how to proceed. The unchanging person is a common occurrence in discipleship contexts, and the reasons for it are worth our consideration.

Cost Counting

> For which of you, desiring to build a tower, does not first sit down and count the cost, whether he has enough to complete it?
>
> (Luke 14:28)

The number of people who want to change is smaller than you may think. Sometimes we forget this as we make our appeals—especially to those we love the most. Though at some level of their hearts, they may want to live a different life. Often, they choose what is familiar because change is hard. Biblical repentance is difficult for all of us, especially with life-habituating patterns. It is like trying to lose weight or trying to quit smoking. What about overcoming fear or anger? What is that one annoying thing you want to change but have not been able to kick the habit? How many of us have tried but found the discipline to rid ourselves of pet addictions more challenging than we first perceived?

A lack of change is a common occurrence among fallen souls. If you do not understand why, you may become frustrated with people stuck in ruts (Galatians 6:1-2). Our responsibility is to water and plant, knowing that no matter how complex things are, God's grace is sufficient for anyone to mature in Christ (Philippians 4:13). There are no problems beyond grace's scope (1 Corinthians 10:13). To say or think my set of issues is different from someone else is denying the power of Christ's death, resurrection, ascension, and mediation (Romans 1:16). Imagine trying to persuade Christ with an excuse for not changing. What could we say?

- "Your grace was not enough."
- "It would help if you did more."
- "I am different, and my situation is unique."

Not recommended! My unwillingness to change is always because of me, not Him or even that woman He gave me. He has provided for me all I need for life and godly living (2 Peter 1:3-4; Philippians 4:19). At some point, I have to realize any lack of change in me is a matter of personal choice, assuming the "thorn" is something that He wants me to change (2 Corinthians 12:7-10). If I choose not to change the changeable, I must examine my excuses. May I share with you seven reasons that have kept me from maturing in Christ? Perhaps you can identify with some of these.

1: I'm Problem-Centered

The gospel is the power of God for salvation and sanctification. Problem-centered, problem-focused people do not perceive this the way they should. Though the answer is right before them, they can be reluctant to submit to God's wonder-working power (Deuteronomy 30:14; Romans 10:8). Through the years, the Lord has sent me a few problem-centered people who did not want to change. Though they would not say they had decided not to change, they did not want to change. They were "the glass is half-empty" people. If you asked them how they were doing, they would give you their list of problems. After a while, the temptation would be to grow weary of them. Grace and gratitude were not part of their everyday speech. It did not matter what you said or what angle you took to turn the conversation toward Christ and His grace, their problems were always too big, and God's solutions were too small.

2: It's My Identity

People stuck in a rut for an extended period can find their identity in the rut. We see this phenomenon in our culture every day. The person is uncomfortable in their skin, so they take on a new identity contrary to biology and the Bible. Rather than changing, they choose an identity comparable to their internal disorderedness. I was talking to a man who had a foster child. The foster child hoards his few belongings in his room while choosing not to play with the other toys his foster parents have provided him. This kid has a squalor identity, which is all he knows. He does not think holding on to his few broken possessions tenaciously is odd. If he continues to live in fear-based thinking after becoming an adult, he will entrench his identity into self-captivating thought patterns (2 Corinthians 10:3–6). A life of freedom, hope, peace, love, grace, and security may be good ideas for others, but not for him.

3: I Want the Quick Fix

One of the most common themes I have seen with unchanging people is their desire for an easy path forward. Like the guy who joined the fitness center in January, but by April, you could not find him with a radar. When some people find out what is involved in the change process, they balk at the opportunity the gracious Lord holds out for them. It's sticker shock! We live in a drive-through, pill-centered culture where everything has to be instant. "I'm not interested if I can't be instantly gratified and satisfied." Sanctification is a cross and a death, not an easy street. Being holy will cost our lives, which does not sell well in suburbia.

Sin interrupts the movers and shakers, looking for a quick fix to keep the dream alive. Sanctification by the sweat of your brow is passé. Legitimately stuck individuals may want to be free, but many do not want to pay the price. It shocks their souls when you tell them about the cost of discipleship. "You can have what you want, but you must die first." (See John 12:24.) One of the ironies with this type of worldview is that they will do whatever it takes in an area of their lives where they want something bad enough while there seems to be no persevering grace when it comes to their sanctification.

> Whoever does not bear his own cross and come after me cannot be my disciple.
> (Luke 14:27)

4: I Like My Sin

We know there is a form of perverse pleasure in sin (Hebrews 11:25). If there were no pleasures in sin, we would not like it. I eat ice cream because I enjoy it. I'm not too fond of mayonnaise because it tastes terrible (Psalm 34:8). Our ultimate loyalty is to ourselves. We are not motivated to choose things we perceive to be unfulfilling. If a person continues to select a sinful habit or lifestyle, it's because they find pleasure in that thing, which is a pleasure that is always greater than a desire to change. They may lament their sad circumstances and even be telling you the truth.

The quiet part they won't say aloud is how much they love their sin or the thing that has entrapped them. For example, the habituated, angry person can talk at length about how bad his anger is and the devastating effects of his verbal rants on others, but there is more to the story. He chooses his sinful anger because he has learned it works for him. It gives him what he wants (James 4:1–3). The choice of sin entices him to choose it as a better option than to do the hard thing, which is to exercise self-control (Galatians 5:22–23). We do what we want, making the angry guy no better than the crack addict; they choose their drug to get what they want.

5: I Fear Freedom

Some people's habituations keep them in bondage for so long that they find a twisted comfort in their prison of pain. My brother was like this. He went to prison when he was seventeen years old. He was released three times. Each time he was released, he would do something illegal to go back. He became an institutionalized convict. The prison was his home. He learned the system and became comfortable with it. People in stressful, long-term situations may whine about their problems but can also be fearful of living a life free from what they have always known.

The world was a big and scary place for my brother. He could not control it, a self-reliant instinct gifted to us by Adam. He could control prison life. He was not afraid of incarceration. He was like the trapeze artist who had to let go of one person to grab hold of another. There is always a moment when he would be holding on to no one. He chose never to let go of what he had—what he could control. A fear-motivated person stuck in dysfunction is not likely to reach out and grab God's hands to be free (Matthew 14:31). He will choose to keep hanging on to what is familiar, never able to fully realize the freedom that is just beyond his fingertips (Galatians 5:1).

6: I Like Attention

My friend's wife committed adultery. She eventually left her husband for another man. Without question, it was the worst season of his life. He spent several years spiritually wandering through confusion and discouragement. I distinctly remember when God's grace was becoming more real to him during that time, and it appeared he might pull through the ordeal. As things began to change for the better, another kind of struggle manifested. It sounded like this:

> If my friends see how much better I am doing, they may leave me alone. I do not want to be alone. The loneliness of being alone is eating away at my soul. I will be measured and cautious about how I communicate how I am doing. I do not want to lose the attention I am getting. Their attention is all I have. It feeds my desire for someone to love me.

Many people knew about his marriage problems, and some sympathized with him. He already felt ostracized because he belonged to a legalistic community that distanced itself from divorced people. Losing his wife was unbearable, but the possibility of his friends not giving him any attention was terrifying. His heart was hurting and plotting. He did not want to trust God to be his only Comforter. He preferred to prolong the perception of pain with superficial caring friends. Lying was better than saying he was okay. He did not want to be left alone. He was like the uncoordinated kid on the sixth-grade basketball team pleading with the jock to "Pick me! Pick me! Please!"

Do not overlook this perverted possibility with unchanging people. We all want attention and accolades, and we typically disdain isolation, even to the point of using pain to create friendships. If your troubles can only garner attention, then troubles may become a way of building a community. People like this can be manipulative in managing and maintaining their tribe. They can also wear out their welcome. In the counseling world, we call them professional counselees. They are forever talking about their problems but never change. If you pulled back the cover on the heart, you might find someone getting their approval drive stroked by their sadistic relishing in their problems.

7: I'm Not Honest

This last group may be the most common. There are many reasons for being dishonest. I just gave you six of them—all of which have a component of deception. Do not be surprised by a person's ability to spin the truth. After you work through the deceit attached to the reasons above, I want you to consider another purpose for lying: they are vetting you. Counseling is a context where people tell many lies. People lie to me all the time. It is kind of sadly humorous at this point in my life. It used to bother me, but I understand my *lying profession* more as I have grown older. People are scared and do not know if you can handle their truth. Thus, they incrementally reveal more and more about themselves.

I remember counseling a young lady who presented herself as a single person. After about two months of counseling, she said she had something she wanted to tell me. I thought she was going to say she had an abortion. I asked her what she wanted to say, and she said she was married. In our first meeting, she said she was single. The whole time I believed she was and counseled her accordingly. I would have never guessed in a million years she was married. She was secretly vetting me. She needed to know if she could trust me with her secrets and if I would steward them well and not judge her as I was bringing biblical help to her.

Call to Action

Caring for people takes a lot of biblical character, capacity, competence, courage, and compassion. You must maintain your biblical equilibrium while emulating the disposition of the Savior. Everybody is not mature or wise enough to filter through the excuses people use for not changing. I trust these few insights have helped you. Here are some questions to assist in your ongoing reflection.

1. Will you pray, asking the Lord to help you to care for others with the patience and compassion of Jesus?
2. Will you offer a prayer of gratitude for the privilege of bringing the gospel to those in bondage to sin?
3. Will you ask Him to help you guide people through their excuses for not changing? What will you do to gain more insight and courage to serve the unchanging person?
4. Will you be as patient with others as God is patient with you? What do you need to change to emulate more patience?
5. As you reflected on these things, were you primarily thinking about yourself or someone else? Why did you answer that way?

7

Expecting Change

In any discipleship situation, the discipler's theology must inform their discipleship process. Theology and application act as guardrails to keep the counseling process moving in the right direction while avoiding the inevitable hazards that inferior theology and deficient applications cause. Maintaining this type of counseling equilibrium has several benefits, such as keeping the discipler from losing hope or even sinning while caring for others. The Bible provides us with a case study to make this point.

Counselor's Temptation

But first, have you ever tried to motivate your child to turn from a destructive behavior only to become frustrated because of his unwillingness to respond to your care humbly? Have you found yourself at your wit's end while trying to come alongside your spouse in hopes change would take place? Have you had similar frustrations with a friend you prayed for or pleaded with to change, but it did not happen? It is not politically correct for a trained biblical counselor, like myself, to admit that biblical counseling has built-in liabilities that set itself up for failure in some counseling situations.

More specifically, I refer to the professional model of formalized biblical counseling, where a counselor meets someone periodically in an official counseling context to work through a situational difficulty. I am not referring to contextualizing biblical counseling in a local church that envisions, equips, and engages the entire church in the model and methods of biblical counseling. However, biblical counseling in a para-church practice or even a local church will have built-in liabilities if the only means of motivating a person to change is the formalized biblical counseling setting conducted by—assumed—trained people. That narrow model for soul care is sub-biblical and a set-up for—at least—four possible inferior outcomes.

- The desired change hoped for may not happen during the expected counseling season.
- If change does not occur, the biblical counselor may lose faith in the change process.
- If change does not take place, the counselee may terminate the process.
- If change does happen, there is no way for the person to receive ongoing care among a community that knows him and has the competency to maintain an appropriate level of care that ensures long-term transformation. The Christian life is repentance and ongoing repenting because some of our problems persist long after addressing them.

The Counseling Window

Many Christians are receiving training to be biblical counselors. Presumably, toward the end of their training, they engage in the wonderful world of biblical counseling with the expectation of seeing lives changed for the glory of God. Undoubtedly, they will see God change many lives through formalized biblical counseling. But to think so narrowly about how and when change happens can make a biblical counselor cynical and pessimistic about why everyone does not change during counseling. This problem occurs when a counselor has an expectation for transformation during a short season of sessions. The implication is clear: "I expect you to change during our prescribed number of counseling sessions."

The New Testament does not teach a formalized "start-stop date" for a specific change in a person's life, making biblical counseling sub-biblical at best. Though change could happen during a counseling window, it is not a New Testament expectation or imperative. Suppose the counselor or the counselee does not discern and guard against this false expectation. In that case, they may embed inherent liabilities in the counseling process that impede progressive sanctification in a person's life. It's akin to parents pressuring kids to change, which could happen externally. However, helping a person at the heart level depends on God granting the prerequisite repentance for that transformation—something no parent or counselor can create.

Another liability is the counselee expecting change to occur during the counseling window. The counselor and counselee hope for the best, a reasonable perspective, but it's incumbent to provide more than lip service to the higher authority and His intentions. God changes hearts while providing the empowering grace needed to mature a person into Christlikeness, but it's not required of Him to do so at our behest. Though there is a responsibility on the discipler to counsel well and the disciple to humbly and practically respond to the discipleship provided, the timing of and power for change comes from the Lord. This non-negotiable fact is why disciplers must guard their hearts against becoming perplexed or frustrated when they do not see transformation according to their preconceived timetable.

Diagnostic Questions

If the discipler does not protect his heart, he will lose faith in the change process for the person he is attempting to help. He will become impatient, possibly rude, harsh, or unkind (1 Thessalonians 5:14). If the discipler does not adjust, he will fall into the ditch of cynicism, suspicion, or even worse, he'll start grumbling and gossiping about the unchanging person. To expound on these counseling hazards, I have eight excellent diagnostic questions to help assess your thoughts about those you want to see change and the process to get there. These questions apply to any soul care provider: parent, child, friend, small group leader, and husband or wife.

- Have you felt yourself losing hope regarding the possibility of a person changing?
- Have you become impatient because of the person's lack of responsiveness?
- Have you ever spoken harshly to a person because they seemed unresponsive to your appeals?
- Have you, through your frustration, shared inappropriate details about someone else?
- Have you felt self-righteous—a greater than/better than attitude—during the discipleship process?
- Have you ever sinned against someone while trying to serve them?
- Based on your experience with a resistant person, have you ever questioned your ability to disciple?
- Have you ever become more focused on your strategies for change than on God's power to bring change?

If you answered yes to any of these questions, it is time to refocus on the only One who can bring authentic change to us. After you examine your heart, you may want to review your discipleship model and the methods within that framework. It may have some inherent liabilities that need your attention. You may find it beneficial to extend your discipleship model and methods to any context where you want the transformation to occur within a specified timetable. This inherent liability can just as accurately be a liability in any discipleship situation, whether you are trying to disciple a friend, family member, or counselee. The essential theological question to start with is your view of the doctrine of repentance. More specifically, do you believe repentance is a gift from God?

Doctrine of Repentance

> And the Lord's servant must not be quarrelsome but kind to everyone, able to teach, patiently enduring evil, correcting his opponents with gentleness. God may grant them repentance leading to a knowledge of the truth, and they may come to their senses and escape from the devil's snare after being captured by him to do his will.
>
> (2 Timothy 2:24–26)

> And the Lord's discipler must not be quarrelsome but kind to all people, able to disciple them, patiently enduring evil, resistance, and ingratitude. When he corrects an individual, he does so with gentleness. Who knows, God may grant them repentance leading to a knowledge of the truth, and they may come to their senses and escape from the devil's snare after being captured by him to do his will.
>
> (RLT Version)

If you believe repentance is a gift from God, you know you cannot conjure, contrive, force, manipulate, or artificially apply it to anyone willy-nilly. We do not will repentance into the heart of an individual regardless of the care context. Armed with this understanding of repentance being a gift from God, you are aware that the implication is that God might not grant it according to your expected timeframe. He might not grant repentance at all. Repentance during a discipleship context is a timing thing. Will God give the gift of repentance while you are discipling this person?

God granted me the gift of repentance while I was an unregenerate twenty-five-year-old. If you tried to disciple me as a rebellious fifteen-year-old, who just landed in jail, you would have potentially been frustrated by my rebellion, stubbornness, and self-deceived thinking. Oh, and don't forget my anger; it could sometimes be intense. But here is the good news: your watering and planting would not have been in vain (1 Corinthians 3:6). Ten years after jail, the Lord decided to grant repentance to me. As I look back, the subordination of human effort to God's kind gift of repentance is evident. What if we applied these thoughts to the prodigal son who has come to you for help? He is angry, bitter, frustrated, and living in rebellion. He just demanded and received a lump of money from his dad and plans to run away from home. Let's look at his case.

A Case Study

He sees himself as a victim. What is common sense to you should be common sense to him. But it isn't. Even his brother is piling on the mess; envy has consumed him, and the prodigal has had enough of all of them. He is now sitting in your counseling office. You've never met him or his family. His daddy asked you to help him. You agree. How would you counsel him if he stumbled through your door? First, let's look at what we know about his story.

- **Luke 15:11:** There was a man who had two sons.
- **Luke 15:12:** And the younger of them said to his father, "Father, give me the share of property that is coming to me." And he divided his property between them.
- **Luke 15:13:** Not many days later, the younger son gathered all he had and took a journey into a far country, and there he squandered his property in reckless living.
- **Luke 15:14:** And when he had spent everything, a severe famine arose in that country, and he began to be in need.
- **Luke 15:15:** So he went and hired himself out to one of the citizens of that country, who sent him into his fields to feed pigs.
- **Luke 15:16:** And he was longing to eat the pods that the pigs ate, and no one gave him anything.
- **Luke 15:17:** But when he came to himself, he said, "How many of my father's hired servants have more than enough bread, but I perish here with hunger!"

Before we get to the end of the story in verse 17, he's sitting with you at verse 12 after receiving a fat stack of Benjamins. He is hunched in a rebellious stupor, angry at his dad, brother, and life. He blames his family for his miserable circumstances and is unwilling to see how the problems consume him or how they all began in his wicked heart (James 4:1–3). As a biblical discipler, your job is to call him to repentance. The facts are clear, and the truth is as obvious as the nose on your face, but he does not repent. According to the Bible story, he does not repent until verse 17. It will be many days—if not years—before he comes to his senses.

Mysterious Repentance

The missing piece of information we do not have is how much time transpired from when he received his money (verse 12) and landed in the hog lot (verse 17). Our best guess is that it was a long time. He received his money. He spent it on reckless living. A famine came upon the land. He went and found a job. He came to his senses. It probably took several months to whittle down his fat stack and for a famine to come upon the land. It could have been a year or more, and though he comes to you in verse twelve, let's say it's one year before he repents of his sins. That is a long time to be counseling someone in a formalized or professional sense of biblical counseling.

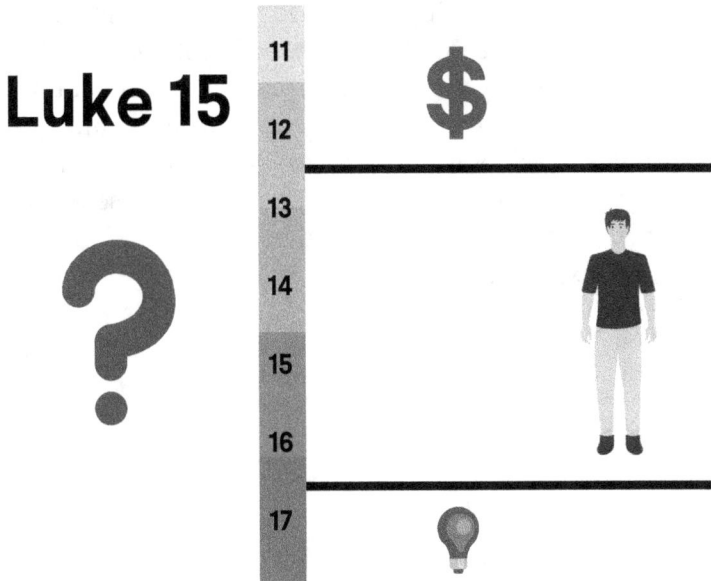

In most cases, the counseling will stall or terminate if a person shows no sign of changing after a short season of meetings. The best thing the counselor can do is water and plant while waiting for God to change the rebel's heart. Repentance is a mystery, only adequately understood in the mind of God (Deuteronomy 29:29). We cannot will it, no matter how adept we are at discipling or caring for people. If the counselor expects to bring the person to a penitent, fruitful, and reconciling conclusion, the counselor would be disappointed. He could have talked to the prodigal until he was blue in the face, but he would not change. It was never God's will for the prodigal to change until verse 17.

The Lord has brought more than one person into my life who came to me months or even years after our initial meetings to thank me for investing in their lives. In those situations, the people were sorrowful for how stubborn and ornery they were during our time together. Sometimes, I became impatient, harsh, unkind, and frustrated with the people because of their resistance to change during my expected time frame. My immature thinking tempted me to put too much hope into the model and method rather than resting in God's mysterious will. I was too self-reliant in my ability to disciple. Other times, I cared for them more than they did. It was not unusual for my fear to feed my advice, which felt more like manipulation on the counselee's end. Rather than resting, trusting, and hoping for God to change hearts, I expected my training and knowledge to make a difference.

Call to Action

1. Will you talk about a friend or family member you manipulated because you were not resting in God's mysterious will for them? What should you have done differently? Is there something you need to do now to make amends for botching up the discipleship time with them? If so, will you do it?
2. Why is it easier to fall into these traps with those we love while being more at rest with those we don't know as well? How will you fortify your heart so that you don't push a loved one too hard?
3. When you think about the gift of repentance, what goes through your mind about those you want to see changed today? What one thing will you do to change yourself so you can avoid the relational trap of over-caring?
4. Is there someone in your life who is not changing? How are you responding to them? Do you need to go to them and repent of impatience, despair, frustration, or something else? If so, will you do that today?
5. Talk about the liability of a para-church or church counseling practice that does not engage and make use of the entire body, which would extend the timeframe for change while creating many more contacts points with the person. What would you do if you had the authority to develop a counseling worldview in your church?

8

A Better Way

Sometimes, when people hear the term biblical counseling, they think about a two-tier system within Christianity: those who can counsel and those who cannot. When I talk to some Christians about biblical counseling, they step back mentally while disqualifying themselves by saying, "I can't do that." For them, biblical counseling connotes a two-tier structure of competency or something for professionals. This problem, among a few other liabilities with the biblical counseling movement, makes it wise to change our thinking about how we do soul care.

Another System

In the last chapter, we pretended the prodigal son was sitting in your counseling office, stewing in anger and rebellion—resisting all your attempts to help him. Because you have read the story (Luke 15:11–17), you know the Lord did not grant the gift of repentance to him until verse 17. But in our pretend story, he comes to you, though he plans to leave home soon to live independently from his family. His departure time is verse 12 of Luke's gospel. During your time with him, you learn many things are awry with his thinking, not to mention his whacked theological perspective.

Your hope is for him to change while meeting with you, but you are working within a traditional biblical counseling window of opportunity; you have six counseling sessions to get him to change his mind. Though you can only speculate, it may be another two years before he comes to an end of himself. The historical biblical counseling model does not work because the prodigal's determination to rebel will outlast your opportunities to encourage him to repent. You goal would be to string out the counseling sessions with him. But you can't. You have a limited watering and planting season.

This situation is where we need a better system for working with people who need our wisdom but are not yet ready to change. It must be a system that can work in the flow of a person's progressive sanctification. Or, if God has not saved them, that system must be able to plod along while being patient as we build the relational bridges to bring the person to Christ. I shared with you my story, which is not an outlier, after getting out of jail. I wanted to change, but the process had to be more than meeting with someone for a series of sessions. It was ten more years become I came to Christ. People with problems, especially life-dominating ones, need long-term soul care in multiple contexts to experience a radical, worldview-shifting transformation.

Timing Is Vital

Traditional biblical counseling is not that system. Perhaps it can be part of a grander model for soul care—a subset of the larger framework. I have been counseling for a long time and can tell you that most counseling does not work in five-and-done or ten-and-done counseling sessions. The unchanging prodigal wants to sow his wild oats while the biblical counselor intends to guide him toward righteous repentance. That's an impasse in the counseling office, and if the counselor is not careful, his plan will press his counselee between a rock and a hard place. There will be a strange tension in the counselor's office as the counselor pushes him to repent while God does not grant him the gift of repentance (2 Timothy 2:24–25).

Have you ever counseled someone, and within the first or second session, they repented and made significant changes in their life? If so, you caught them in verse 17 of Luke's gospel (Luke 15:17). They received the gift of repentance from God, and you just happened to be sitting in front of them when He granted it. That does not happen often, but when it does, it makes counseling a pleasant experience for everyone. Years ago, an adulterous lady told me I was an excellent counselor. She came to me for counseling, and through the counseling process, she changed. Eventually, she repented and jumped on the road to Christian maturity. I did not tell her what I was thinking.

The truth is that I am not that great of a counselor. I just happened to be in front of her when God broke into her stubborn, cold heart. It was my lucky day, and hers too. God granted repentance. There was a reason the fifteen previous counselees I met would not change: God did not give them repentance. After the Lord granted repentance, she humbled herself, received His grace, repented of her sin, and began to change her life. Let's give credit where credit is due. It was because the good Lord brought her to her senses. He chose to grant the adulterous counselee repentance. From that point forward, it was like painting by numbers. Any counselor will be an excellent counselor when the counselee decides to change.

The Best Context

Biblical counselors can put too much pressure on themselves to fix people if the counselor's understanding of the Lord's role in counseling is inadequate or they do not include the local church in the person's process for change. If the counselor does not have a vital discipleship church context, the counseling will have built-in liabilities, which will be a set-up for unnecessary frustration for everyone. People ask if I do biblical counseling at my church. That is a trick question. I do biblical counseling at my church because I am a Christian. Every church member is a biblical counselor, whether they know it or do it like me because the Bible assumes every church member is a Christian.

The issue here is not whether I am for biblical counseling. I am! I love biblical counseling. I'm trained to do biblical counseling. I pursued my ACBC Fellowship because of my affection for biblical counseling. I started this ministry to spread my passion for biblical counseling to the Christian community. My love for biblical counseling is strong, but I have a greater appreciation for the New Testament local church doing the work of soul care—what the Bible has always assumed as discipleship. Because of my affection for the local church, I want to go the extra mile in not creating or implying a two-headed model for discipleship within the local church.

All biblical counselors believe that every Christian should participate in the counseling process at some level of their hearts. Jay Adams has served us well in communicating this truth since his groundbreaking work in 1970. His book Competent to Counsel set a new trajectory for the local church's total involvement in counseling (Romans 15:14). He repackaged and re-launched the idea of counseling in a compelling way that has served multiplied thousands of churches. Though God has used Jay to do this fantastic work, I have observed too many local churches lacking total engagement in a comprehensive view of counseling practice—called discipleship, the very thing Jay said we should be doing.

Let's Reclassify

Though everyone can and should care for others, most of the heavy lifting of counseling happens among a few people rather than all the people. Part of the reason for this is that biblical counseling has taken on a life within the local church over the past few decades. In some ways, it has mutated into an extension of the church or para-help that comes alongside the church to assist because the church is deficient in the sanctification process, or, even worse, they don't know how to do soul care. Part of the reason for this is the reclassification of the counseling process. Biblical counseling has become the new appellation we map over the more appropriate and biblical term discipleship. Many people see the two terms as two different needs for the Christian.

Biblical counseling has unintentionally weakened the function of discipleship in the local church. It would be better to rename, restate, or reclassify biblical counseling according to its biblical roots. Biblical counseling, by definition, is too narrow of a term to encompass what we should be doing. The term connotes a specialist or trained individual who is a professional. The word can also lead a person to believe the average Christian is not qualified to bring counsel to someone else. Though we need some specificity, precision, and training in the discipleship process for specific situations, we are shooting ourselves in the foot if we do not broaden what it means to care for each other. We must envision the entire church. Everyone should participate in the "counseling process" at some level, according to the person's God-given gift.

Instead of calling what we do counseling, let's call it discipleship. Discipleship is more nuanced and gets into the nooks and crannies of the local church's sanctification model. We do not want to reduce the number of people doing discipleship or set up unnecessary artificial contexts (counseling sessions) that can manipulate or attempt to press righteousness on a person prematurely. This self-imposed pressure for holy living creates non-God-ordained timelines for change. My earlier reframing of the story about the prodigal illustrates the liability of attempting to press for righteousness in an artificial context. I long for the day when discipleship reclaims its biblical heritage by taking over biblical counseling through the engagement of the entire local church in a fully orbed, powerful, one-another-body ministry.

Discipleship's Advantages

There is a substantial philosophical and methodological difference between counseling the prodigal son in a counseling context versus spending time with him at different points along his journey. It's called doing life in the milieu: meeting him in the social environments in which he is living. Practicing discipleship has many more advantages than biblical counseling. One of those advantages is it does not press the issue of repentance on a person but is pneumatic (Spirit-led), which builds, plods, speaks, comforts, convicts, and changes. Discipleship and counseling are as different as the tortoise and the hare. The tortoise is poised, strategic, deliberate, well-paced, and systematic. The hare has a job to do; it is about getting it done as fast as possible.

The hare may also be strategic and methodical, but therein lies the problem: his strategy is to accomplish the task today because counseling is not an open-ended arrangement or expectation, which can put counseling at odds with God's plan of repentance for the person. But if you practice discipleship rather than counseling, you know it is easier to keep a person "in a church building" rather than trying to get him to come back to an artificial context for change, like a counseling office. Loving a person is easier while doing life with him rather than trying to love him during a counseling session where you call him to repentance every time you meet. How exasperating! You can only do this for so long before it strains the relationship—

to the point of breaking it off. There are more advantages to discipleship in the local church when the entire church body is engaged.

- The church can love and serve the prodigal.
- The church can love and care for his family.
- The church can model the life of Christ before him.
- The church can connect other members of the body to all of them.
- The church can provide hospitality.
- The church can provide a small group for them.
- The church can do lunch with them.
- The church can plan fun events with them.
- The church can engage them at the weekly church meeting.
- The church can provide biblical counseling.
- The church can patiently wait and pray for the Lord to grant repentance.

That's a shortlist. What if you added five more just for the fun of it? No biblical counselor can provide this many things for anyone or his family. Suppose you can keep a person in the church building long enough. In that case, the likelihood of him repenting in God's good and kind providence is more likely than five-and-done counseling sessions while sending them away with no regular follow-up or connectivity to the body of Christ.

In the Building

"Keeping him in the building" is not a static responsibility. It is spontaneous and structured. It consistently provides love and care for those who need to change, grow, and mature in Christ. The counseling office has a singular focus: "I need you to change soon." Discipleship in the context of the local church is a more relaxed environment. It permits people to live in the gospel's good while coming alongside each other, helping them to follow their examples (Ephesians 5:1; 1 Corinthians 11:1; Philippians 4:9). Discipleship is hard work. It is not for the lazy person. All hands are on deck, and everyone is busy thinking about living in the good of the gospel while inviting others into their faith walk with Christ.

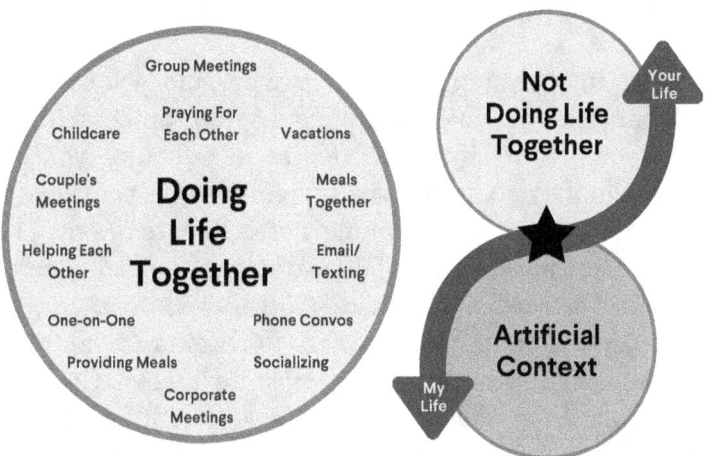

Counseling has a counselor sitting in a chair, instructing another person on how to live for Christ. Discipleship is about doing real life with another human being while speaking into his life along the way, which is how Christ did it. The counselor's challenge is building a robust relational bridge to tell the hard truth of God's Word in love (Ephesians 4:15). The counseling context is almost like picking someone out of a crowd, sitting them down, and bringing complex corrections to them. Most discipleship happens between close friends. Most counselors are in the unenviable position of correcting someone they hardly know. Here is my tongue-in-cheek, five-step approach to biblical counseling between two people who do not have a prior relationship with each other:

1. "Hello, I'm Rick. Please tell me your name."
2. "Wonderful! Now tell me why you are here."
3. "I love you very much!"
4. "You are making a big mistake and continuing down your current path would be foolish."
5. "Will you come back next week so we can continue our discussion?"

Though my five-step approach is hyperbole, you can sense the liabilities intrinsic to the counseling process. To add to this and to heighten the degree of difficulty, you have approximately sixty minutes to demonstrate your love for the counselee while bringing correction to them. (This time problem is one reason I have always counseled for two hours.) You have sixty minutes to get to know them, love them, give them hope, call them to repentance, and hope to create a desire in them to return next week. Good luck with that weak model for progressive sanctification if it is outside a sanctification center—the local church. The local church discipleship process has a different setup. It can include specific, one-to-one discipleship opportunities, but it can do so much more. It has been my experience that if the whole church lived a gospel-centered life, there would not be much need for all the formalized counseling we see today.

Call to Action

1. Why is a discipleship model in the local church context a better approach to help folks change than an isolated counseling model?
2. Traditional biblical counseling can be a subset of the grander discipleship methodology, but if it is not, what are some of the liabilities of a stand-alone counseling ministry?
3. If you work within a narrow biblical counseling framework, disconnected from a comprehensive model for discipleship in the local church, how will you help those you counsel to maintain their transformation after you stop meeting with them?
4. Is your local church coming alongside you to help you with the soul care of those you hope will change? If not, why not?
5. Are you doing your part as a Christian counselor (discipler) in your church? If not, why not?
6. What would need to change in your church to make it a more effective sanctification center?

9

Forcing Change

Will you test yourself before you read this chapter? What are your thoughts toward those you would like to see change, especially those not responding the way you hoped they would? My aim is for you to consider the motives and methods you employ when motivating someone to change. If we do not have a proper motive, it will affect our methods, even tempting us to demand or manipulate someone to change while never considering how out of tune we are with God and the narrative He is writing for the unchanging person.

Patient with All

As you reflect on my question, will you consider these two also? Are you generally impatient toward the person you want to see change? Are you easily frustrated, critical, unforgiving, bitter, or fearful toward an unchanging person? There are more questions I could ask, but these are enough to help you assess your heart toward those you care about and want to assist. If our hearts are not right toward those in our care, the first thing for us to change is ourselves. We cannot export what we don't possess; if we're not right with God, whether it's our motive or method, we may botch our efforts to help them get right with God.

Being redemptive in other people's lives starts in our hearts, not theirs. If your habit is to assess your heart before you speak, you're in a great spot. James talked about being "slow to speak," a great discipline when discipling folks. I work to be that way with others, especially my family members. The people in our care are unlike us, and God is doing something different in their lives. The common temptation is to map our experiences over them, accelerating our expectations for them, which can sabotage our best efforts. Let me explain with my friend Biff.

Biff knows how to get things done. He is a successful guy. His reputation and business are well-known in the community. People like him and come to him to learn his secret sauce for success. On the surface, nothing is wrong with what you see in Biff, but after you get to know him, you do not want to partake in his secret sauce. Biff is a controller who demands his employees do things his way. His methods work because his employees need a job. They will put up with Biff as long as he pays them well. So, Biff keeps churning along, raking in the dough. Though he is a "success" on the business front, he is a frustrated and unsuccessful husband, father, and friend. His work methods do not export well to his home life. His attempts to motivate his family members are poorly received because they are more forced than nurtured. His lack of success in the home confuses Biff because he knows he is right. For example, he wants a loving wife and obedient children.

Plant and Water

Biff told me, "What's wrong with that? This is what God wants." I responded, "It may be what God wants, but God does not force righteousness on anyone. The Lord creates contexts of grace and invites people into those spaces while motivating them with grace." The "hardcore law method" that Biff is implementing does not motivate people to change—at least not for the right reasons or in long-term, sustainable ways. His methods do the opposite:

they discourage and exasperate people. The Lord's "grace method" motivates people to choose righteousness. God does not demand our obedience or impose it upon us as though the only thing that matters is results. The Lord keeps the end goal in mind (Hebrews 12:1-2), using biblical methods that lead to that end.

> Or do you presume on the riches of his kindness and forbearance and patience, not knowing that God's kindness is meant to lead you to repentance?
> (Romans 2:4

Our loving, heavenly Father could have accomplished His purposes for us without us. I suppose. He could have made us righteous, but by doing so, it would have marginalized our relationship with Him. Our relationships would be more robotic than human/divine reciprocality. Biff prefers the robot approach with his employees and family. He wants hard-wired hired hands to accomplish his goals—a strategy that is blowing up his family. His employees won't leave because they need a job, but his children are not as obligated or bound. They won't leave now because they are young, and his wife is unwilling to divorce—at least not today.

Biff has put his family between a rock and a hard place. The "rock" is that he wants them to be how he legislates. The hard place is how they resist what he wants, and he cannot legislate his mandates. The tension in the home moves between uneasy peace and explosive anger. It has yet to occur to Biff how his outcome was never meant to be his to determine (1 Corinthians 3:6). God has not called us to determine the outcome with people but to trust Him for those results, even if the results are not to our liking. God has called us to faithfully and gratefully work the process while leaving the outcome to Him. The problem is that Biff wants to plant, water, and manage, manipulate, and mandate the growth. James would call Biff arrogant. (See James 4:13-16.)

Do As I Say

A man who tries to control the process and the outcome does not need God because he is a god. There is no room in Biff's world for God because Biff has everything under control—at least, that is the illusion he wants to perpetuate. The problem is that Biff is not a good god. Many of his employees are angry with him, his wife is mad at him, and his children are growing in resentment by the day, which will turn into rebellion once they become courageous enough to share their true thoughts with him. This tragedy happens in many marriages and family debacles when one person—usually a parent—believes they know how things should be.

They mandate the outcome based on their belief, inevitably leading to disaster. I suspect most of the time, the parent is correct in what they believe and want to do, though their rightness is not in debate here. The problem is when the parent tries to mandate righteousness on the family. The parent may be sincerely trying to avert dangers and disasters they see gathering on the horizon of the child's life, but legislating morality is a multifaceted problem that needs divine perspective and intervention. Parents are not omniscient: they do not have God's full mind on the issues (Isaiah 55:8-9). The legislative parent does not understand how God can use sin sinlessly to accomplish His good purposes (Genesis 50:20).

Self-reliance rather than God-reliance is a natural temptation for all parents (2 Corinthians 1:8-9). Parents genuinely do not want their loved ones to suffer, a prospect that is impossible to avoid (Genesis 3:7-19). Some parents have yet to learn how God perfects His strength in our weaknesses. Sometimes God has to weaken a child to display His power through the child (2 Corinthians 1:8-9, 4:7, and 12:7-10). Biff can get away with his tactics and strategies at work because his employees will do things his way, or they will leave. Biff has bought into his culture's view of success. It's called a *win*. (Jesus dying on a tree was a "win" too.) Biff can't get away with running roughshod over his family. His bad habits create a blind spot. His reaction leaves him with three options: hire robots, change how he treats people, or continue living in familial dysfunction while alienating himself from everyone important to him.

Robot for Hire

If he hires robots for work and marries one for home, he can program them to do what he wants. It would be a "perfect" world. If there were anything he did not like about his Robo World or if he made a mistake (not likely) or came to understand things differently (an anomaly), he could upgrade to 2.0, 3.0, or 4.0. He could create an infinite number of iterations to have new and improved workers, an ever-improving wife, and always compliant children. He could accomplish his goals with little relational angst, effort, or challenges. Of course, there is at least one problem with this schema: God wants relationships, not robots for hire, even though the Lord knew those relationships would always be messy.

God understands the doctrines of salvation and progressive sanctification. He will take any person at any time—just as they are—and relate to them in such a way that motivates them toward change. He also gives us room to wobble. The Lord patiently works the change process without mandating artificial timelines for change. Though He is a bottom-line Being: He wants Christlike results; He is aware of the process. One of the blessings here is how it deepens our relationship with God. The ongoing process of change gives Him opportunities to demonstrate His love to us, even while we are imperfectly following Him (Romans 5:8; 1 Corinthians 11:1). He does not respond to us according to what we deserve; He provides love ad infinitum (Psalm 103:10–14; Romans 5:8).

Playing in the Dirt

The word Adam means red man or man of the dirt (Genesis 2:7). We are dust (Psalm 103:14). I am a dirt clod, and you are too. The Lord knows this because He created Adam. God loves playing in the dirt, and He knows His audience intimately well (John 2:24-25). He knows life is not about present perfection but a process that matures within a context of loving leadership that moves us into ever-unfolding Christlikeness. Do you see dirty friends and family members as opportunities to cooperate with God to shape them for His glory (2 Corinthians 4:7)? Are you tempted to manipulate the clay pots in your life according to your preferences rather than trusting the Lord?

> And we urge you, brothers, admonish the idle, encourage the fainthearted, help the weak, be patient with them all.
> (1 Thessalonians 5:14)

Paul talked about people differences when he wrote to the Thessalonians. He wanted to make sure they understood how different people are and how treating everybody the same way would be wrong. 1 Thessalonians 5:14 has three people groups: the unruly, the small-souled, and the physically or mentally challenged. Also, notice how he closes his appeal by saying they should be patient with all of them. Paul was not talking about the result but the process of imperfect plodding people making their way toward what we hope would be Christlikeness.

Paul's appeal is even more critical regarding our wives, children, close friends, and our local churches. Everybody is different; each person requires specialized and customized attention. Cooperating with God in the transformation of others is a fantastic honor. Suppose our primary focus is the result of the process, and our methods do not matter.

In that case, there is a good chance we will miss the blessing of engaging our friends in mutually beneficial transformational opportunities that will elevate the fame of Jesus while maturing our relationships.

Addendum for Spouses

Did you know your spouse is a double-damaged person? Your spouse was born in sin and had parents born in sin. It's a double-whammy—coming from Adam and parented by Adamic people. You received double damaged goods when you married your spouse. No matter how great their parents were, they were not perfect, and your spouse did not arrive at the altar entirely sanctified. More than likely, there are traces of residual problems that Adam and their parents caused, making it vital that you become a student of your spouse so you can cooperate with God in the redemptive narrative He is writing for your spouse.

Too often, the newly wedded person expects things from their spouse without carefully discerning the damaged goods they married, with the purpose of discipling them into Christlikeness. Sometimes a spouse says, "This is not what I signed up for." I must ask, "And you signed up for what? A perfect spouse or a work-in-progress?" Your spouse is a dirt clod. Suppose you are demanding a result without helping them achieve the goal of glorifying God. In that case, you need to rethink your motives and methods while recalibrating your perspectives to something more aligned with God's Word.

Call to Action

It would be best never to alter the biblical change process to reach your goal. It does not work that way. Maybe you're right in what should happen, but the process to get to that good end might not be the path you would choose. Perhaps these few helpful questions will assist in your reflections about how change works and be something you can apply to anyone you're discipling.

1. How are you creating a context of grace in your relationship that is conducive to the sanctification and growth of the person you're helping?
2. What resentment, bitterness, or unforgiveness are you harboring against someone you want to see changed but who is not heeding your appeals?
3. In what ways have you demanded changes without entering into the complicatedness of his or her world or discerning the Lord's mind for this person?
4. Are you aware that even if you are right, the result you hope for may not happen? How do you usually respond to those who are not doing what you ask them to do? Are you resting and trusting or demanding and manipulating? Is there something you must address with God and the person you're attempting to help? If so, what is your plan to change?

10

Consider This

If you know someone who is not changing, do not despair. There is a way to help them. I'm not suggesting they will change even if you did everything perfectly, but there is a process for transformation that every Christian should know. I will break down those dynamics of change for you—the essential elements to lead someone into Christlike transformation. I hope the Lord will use these thoughts as you serve those you love so well.

Effects of Hiding

Biff was living in secret sin. Biff is a Christian. He did not tell anyone about his secret for many months, and the longer he held on to it, the more frustrated, relationally distant, and internally hardened he became. It appears that Paul was correct when he said God's wrath rains down from heaven against anyone who presses His truth from their lives. For Biff, his life became unbearable even for him, though he doubled down to keep the masquerade going. Keep moving forward when your plan is going badly, hoping things will change eventually. It's the golfer's fantasy, always believing you'll straighten it out on the next hole. Biff was living inside his personal golfer's fantasy.

> For the wrath of God is revealed from heaven against all ungodliness and unrighteousness of men, who

> by their unrighteousness suppress the truth.
> (Romans 1:18)

Eventually, the hidden sin did come to light, which was mercy from the Lord because Biff had no intention of telling anyone about what he was doing. Sin will always ravage the soul if left unattended because it is not a neutral force. It is a living and active agent that captures the heart while leaving its victims calloused and blind (Hebrews 4:7). You could say Biff was a modern-day David. Sin's purpose is to penetrate the soul to destroy the inner person (John 10:10). The spirit, mind, will, emotions, conscience, thoughts, intentions, and motives become gnarled, ravaged, and conquered. As a midwestern town after a tornado, sin does not take prisoners. It kills them. David captured the effects on the soul of the person who keeps quiet about their nefariousness.

> For when I kept silent, my bones wasted away through my groaning all day long. For day and night your hand was heavy upon me; my strength was dried up as by the heat of summer.
> (Psalm 32:3-4)

Complete Repentance

Have you ever considered how the Lord is part of sin's assault on our souls? Carefully reflect on what Paul said in Romans 1:18. God rains down His wrath on anyone who pushes His truth out of their lives. Nobody—believer or unbeliever—can escape the displeasure of God or the distortions of sin if they don't want to come clean. David felt the wrathful anger of the Lord as well as the deteriorating effects of wrongdoing during his silence. Biff was also slowly dying on the vine (John 15:5) because of his choice to keep quiet. Sin's deception had clouded his judgment.

Repentance is only sweet to the humble soul, and the person who has experienced the gift of repentance (2 Timothy 2:25) always testifies to its blessedness. David came around to the blessedness of repentance eventually.

> Blessed is the one whose transgression is forgiven, whose sin is covered. Blessed is the man against whom the LORD counts no iniquity, and in whose spirit there is no deceit.
> (Psalm 32:1–2)

What is repentance? What does it look like, practically speaking? What are the steps? Perhaps it would help to think about the order of salvation (Ordo Salutis), which also has steps. If you stretch the word salvation to peer inside, you'll see a linkage of beautiful portraits hanging on the walls of a magnificent museum we call salvation. There is a similar linkage to repentance, an order to repentance (Ordo Poenitentiae). I have placed those elements sequentially to show how we should interact with them so that complete and effectual change can happen for anyone. There are thirteen links in the repentance chain.

1. Sin
2. Guilt
3. Conviction
4. Confession
5. Pre-forgiveness
6. Forgiveness
7. Post-forgiveness
8. Reconciliation
9. Restoration
10. Put off the old person
11. Renew the mind
12. Put on a new person
13. Disciple others

Consider This

Repentant Living

Complete repentance is not any of those things but all of them—one at a time in sequential order. You will know if you have changed after you go from a sinning, self-focused lifestyle to a redemptive others-centered lifestyle (Philippians 2:3-5). Our lack of working through all the elements of repentance explains why we live in recurring sin patterns. The Christian life consists of "repentance and ongoing repenting," a redemptive lifestyle that makes any person, friend, family, or church dynamic. We will never fully repent because we cannot attain perfection in the here and now, making repentance living a necessity to live well with God, self, and others.

Every Christian should have a solid functional knowledge of repentance and an active lifestyle compatible with that knowledge. Long-term, progressive, sustainable change will not happen without practical Bible knowledge and authentic biblical engagement. As with all journeys, how you begin determines how you will continue throughout the process, plus your end point. Do you want to end well? Start well and maintain biblical expectations throughout your journey. This need in our lives is why it's essential to understand all the elements in the order of repentance. For now, I will focus on two specific aspects of repentance—conviction and confession.

After we sin, there will be guilt from God. This guilt does not require acknowledgment or acceptance because we do not determine the lines of transgression. Guilt is not a feeling but a forensic fact: God declares us guilty (Genesis 2:16-17; Romans 5:12, 6:23). Though we can twist sin to mean whatever we want it to mean, we cannot change what God says about His righteous morality. When I sin, I am guilty before God. I can dance around it, make excuses, or point out the faults of others, but none of those things reduce the guilt or change God's opinion about what I did.

Deflecting Sin

The only correct answer to guilt is confession, born out of conviction, but sometimes the transgressor chooses one of sin's allies. There are several of them. For example, blame is a standard deflection. It excuses my actions by placing the reason on another person or thing. Then there is justification, which is declaring myself not guilty by saying, "I am not wrong for what I did." Some folks rationalize: "It's not a big deal; everybody is doing it." There is such a normalization of sin in our culture that many people do not have proper biblical categories as they unwittingly rationalize their actions. Of course, there is alleviation when the wrath of God rains from heaven, tempting the transgressor to escape through addictive behaviors, i.e., binge-watching, shopping, eating, porn, drugs, etc.

These deflections are like someone standing before the judge in traffic court. They were driving too fast. The speeder makes much of what the other drivers did while never owning what he did. It's smoke and mirrors. It is game-playing. It's intellectual dishonesty, a more pleasant way of saying the person is either willfully lying or self-deceived. Self-deception is the precondition for the conscience to blur the lines in a person's mind between right and wrong, leading to the use of deflections.

It is incredible for the Lord to send conviction immediately on the heels of our guilt. Conviction is our way of feeling (or experiencing) God's guilt over what we have done wrong. This experience is what David was talking about in Psalm 32. He felt the Lord's guilt, a heavy conviction for what he did, affecting him spiritually and physically. I suspect David felt this weight because of his profound affection for God. He had a massive heart for the Lord. The higher your love is for God, the more significantly you will feel the weight of your sin. The opposite is also accurate.

Heartfelt Agreement

To be desensitized to sin is a dangerous place to be. Paul discussed this in 1 Timothy 4:2 when he wrote about the seared conscience. To sin repeatedly without genuine repentance is the beginning of a layering effect where you can no longer feel the conscience. There is a quenching of the Spirit (1 Thessalonians 5:19). It grieves Him (Ephesians 4:30). If a person does not feel conviction for sin, he will not be motivated to confess his sin, which is the fourth step in the Ordo Poenitentiae: sin, guilt, conviction, and confession. To confess is to agree with God (and anyone else) about what you did.

True confession cannot happen if we do not experience Spirit-given conviction because we won't be able to confess the sin committed if we're unaware of our guilt. One of the instructive things I have observed in Christianity is a process of repentance that marginalizes conviction. You can hear it by the casualness with which a person talks about what they did wrong. When David confessed his sin, he felt conviction, which communicated humbled brokenness over his actions. Though every confession should not read like Psalm 51, every confession should be heartfelt.

It's not good to frame our confession in a casual "I'm sorry" or "Will you forgive me for what happened" Christian speak that follows a formula where there is a detached heart from the spoken words. That is not a person engaged in the change process. That is someone doing damage control over the situation or a conflict resolution technique that preserves the reputation of the transgressor. The wording of our confession must be more than Bible-sounding Christian-speak. I'm not suggesting confession must be overly-emotive, but heartfelt is heart-explained, and you hear it in David's confession.

Weak Forgiveness

The concern here is whether we are humbly engaging God and others so we can effectively turn from what we have done. You may have seen this "kind of repentance" in a child.

1. "Son, did you sin against your sister?"
2. "Yes, dad."
3. "What do you need to do, son?"
4. "Say, 'I'm sorry.'"
5. "Well? Are you going to say it?"
6. "I'm sorry."
7. "What else, son?"
8. To his sister, "Will you forgive me?"
9. "What are you going to say to your brother?"
10. "I forgive you."

That confession and forgiveness scenario directed by the dad is performative. Perhaps it's necessary to teach the children how to do it, but Christians must do better than formulaic Christian speak. The Spirit of God motivates us to feel God-given conviction for what we did wrong. We may inwardly smile as our children walk through a false repentance scenario, but it is a much bigger problem when Christians learn the language, but there is no noticeable difference in our repentance and how children do it. You might as well train your parrot to do it because it will save time.

The weight of conviction you feel over your sin will be proportional to your love for the person you hurt. This aspect of conviction will be problematic for some people because there are folks they have sinned against that they do not love or do not love well. Think about it this way. When you lose something you love, you feel the weight of that loss, a concept that applies to any cherished treasure or relationship (Ephesians 5:29). When you damage that thing or a person you love in any way, you feel it.

Sinner, Meet Gospel

Every loving parent feels genuine love when their child is hurt or, in some cases, dies. The pain you feel in your heart is proportional to your love for that child. Conviction is a form of grief you have for someone who is hurting. In the early part of our marriage, I could sin against my wife and blow it off as though it was not a big thing. I could do this because I had underlying anger and unforgiveness toward her. I was a bitter husband. It was even more damning because I could blame, justify, or rationalize my actions away. Deflections made it easy for me to sin against Lucia and then make excuses while never truly owning what I did wrong.

There were times when I said, "I'm sorry," or even, "Will you forgive me," but those words were not born out of a broken heart (convicted) over my sin against her (and God). Then the Lord introduced me to the gospel, which opened my eyes to see what a low-down, dirty, rotten sinner I was. My soul began to sink into the worthlessness (Romans 3:12) of my depravity as the Lord was simultaneously lifting me by realizing the riches of His mercy (Ephesians 2:1–10). My self-righteousness turned into vapor, which opened a portal to see my wife in a new light.

Rather than belittling or being mean to her, I became grateful for the Lord's gift: I did not deserve His salvation or my wife. She became my treasure, and to sin against her created brokenness that I had never felt up to that time. If you feel little conviction about your nastiness toward someone, your love for them is minimal, and your process of repentance will fizzle out. David was a man after the Lord's heart (Acts 13:22), which explains why the weight of his sin was killing him. I am unsure how long David could have continued his sin if Nathan had not confronted him (2 Samuel 12:1–13).

Call to Action

I would like for you to discuss these questions with a friend. If you are not a conviction-feeling repenter, ask the Lord to help you see what you may not be able to see right now and to feel the weight of your wrongs so you can effectually change.

1. When you sin, how broken are you? Do you feel the weight of your actions to the degree that you are motivated to make them right, regardless of the cost (Luke 15:17–20)? What will you change about yourself if you do not feel the weight?
2. Do you skip conviction like a child by going into "I'm sorry" or "Will you forgive me" mode without meaning it? Are you more about conflict resolution and damage control than genuine repentance? If so, how will you change?
3. Is there anyone you have sinned against for whom you refuse to ask forgiveness? If so, your sin against them and God is more significant than your love for them or God. Will you go to them as soon as you can?
4. How do you need to change from what you have read? Will you make a plan for change and share it with a friend?

Consider This

11

Four Steps to Change

Because of the clarity of God's Word, the path to life change is not mysterious or elusive. If it were complex, we'd all be in a mess. Did you know that Paul gave his protégé, Timothy, a practical plan for change that we can replicate in our lives too? Though Paul's process is not the final or plenary word for transformation, it's one of the most excellent thumbnail sketches you'll find in Scripture. It's concise, understandable, and, best of all, attainable. But first, may I share a story about how change happens in a child's mind?

Christian Life Plan

"Dad, why do you counsel someone so long?"

—Daughter

"Because it takes a while to help them change."

—Dad

"It seems that it would only take a minute. You say, 'Repent;' the person changes, and that is all you have to do. What else do you talk about with them?"

—Daughter

We smile, though our daughter does have a point, which can cause one to wonder how much relational conflict and dysfunction we could eliminate if we followed her approach. I'm sure it wouldn't clean up all our messes, but it would probably make a dent in some of the junk we spread amongst our relationships. Because repentance is not native to us, God is patient as He comes alongside us to teach us how to change. After Adam first sinned, he decided not to repent, blaming his problems on someone else (Genesis 3:12). Have you ever tried that? As sons and daughters of Adam, blaming, rationalizing, or justifying problems away are the things that tempt us as we adjust our fig leaves (Genesis 3:7).

Mercifully, God perseveres with us by not allowing us to stay tangled in our sinful isolation, creating a duality—who we are versus the person we present to others, hoping they might like that version better (Galatians 6:1). One of the primary means of grace the Lord uses to help us change is His Word. For example, when Paul was teaching his young pastor friend, he highlighted how God uses His Word to change us by laying out a four-step plan for change. My intent is not to be as simple as our daughter by suggesting this is all you need, but this working thumbnail will stick with you for life if you make it yours by applying it.

Elements to Change

> All Scripture is breathed out by God and profitable for teaching, for reproof, for correction, and for training in righteousness, that the man of God may be complete, equipped for every good work.
> (2 Timothy 3:16–17)

The words I want to focus on are teaching, reproof, correction, and training. I realize the point of the passage highlights and elevates God's inspired-sufficient-plenary-authoritative Word. My aim is not to devalue the text's purpose, but I want to turn it over again and look at it more practically. What if we highlight these four elements of change that Paul laid out for Timothy? What if we applied them to our lives? If you try this at home, I promise it will change your family dynamics. So, let's begin with teaching and roll slowly through the other three while asking ourselves a few insightful questions along the way to ensure we're making those tweaks that will glorify God, change us, and impact our relationships.

After God had regenerated you—assuming you are a Christian, He began to teach you His Word—a process of recurring illumination, instruction, conviction, and transformation, called progressive sanctification (John 17:17). God's Word is one of the primary means for us to mature into Christlikeness. Through contexts and people, the Word of God penetrates our hearts for personal transformation. If we follow Paul's prescriptive progression in this passage, we will notice how the use of God's Word is to stop dangerous thinking by reorienting our minds to sound teaching. As noted in the Timothy template, the Lord terminates inadequate teaching by reproving us.

The word reprove means to knock us down. The idea here is that the Lord brings sound teaching into our lives to put us on our backsides. We begin to see the light through the Spirit's illuminating conviction (1 John 1:7-10). How often has God brought His Word to you to stop you from your course of action? Though sometimes God's adjustments can be inconvenient and even painful, it is His mercy to care so much about us. He wants to change us. Before I proceed, will you take some time to assess yourself to see how well you are responding to Paul's first two points regarding the change process? The Word of God is profitable for teaching and rebuking. Here are some helpful questions for you and your friends regarding your teachableness and receptivity to rebuke.

Teaching

- Are you teachable? Ask a friend if you are easy to teach. If you have a spouse, ask them about your teachability. Do you create an environment of grace where they can step into it and teach you?
- Is it easy for people to care for you because of your hunger for the Bible's teaching? Are you more concerned about learning than your reputation? Do you recognize that what you don't know outpaces what you do know, so you're eager to learn?
- Do you seek those you trust and are competent enough to teach you? Polling ignorant people is not wise, so you're looking for those farther down the sanctification path.
- Are you a question-asker? Do you pursue others with questions about how to change your life while not succumbing to the temptation of letting their opinions manage you? Are you oversensitive? Does your insecurity hinder people from speaking into your life?

Because teaching is the door through which you will grow, it is incumbent upon you to be teachable. You will not be able to change your life if you are not teachable, the first step in the change process. Your teachability is the litmus test that will inform others about your seriousness to growing in Christ. If you're unteachable, perhaps there will be those who want to care for you, but the sign on the door is clear: No Trespassing.

Rebuking

- Are you a rebukeable person? Can you receive the corrective observations of others? When someone reproves you, how do you initially respond? Are you more focused on the person who said it and how they

said it or on how you can humbly react to it?
- Are you tempted to sulk or go into self-pity mode after someone reproves you? If so, what does your response tell you about your relationship with God? Why is He not all-sufficient and all-sustaining in your life? Perhaps fear of man is in play, and you're permitting the opinions of others to control you.
- Do you express gratitude to those who love you enough to bring correction into your life? You can measure your relational wealth by the number of friends you invite into your corrective care sphere. All parents should be shepherding their children to become part of this sphere as they mature.

Being reproved or rebuked is tough stuff. Nobody enjoys it. To be willing to have others speak into your life is one of the high marks of Christian maturity. Rebukeable people typically have humble and wise perspectives about themselves. They are rebukeable because the gospel rightly informs them. (See Romans 3:10–12, 23, 5:12; Isaiah 64:6; 1 Timothy 1:15.) Being informed by the gospel means they were in a helpless and worthless condition before the Lord chose to save them. They were dead in their sins, hell-bound, and outside God's grace (Ephesians 2:1–10). Alienated from life in God was their spiritual condition (Ephesians 4:18).

Bad Precedes Good

The Lord's view of you before salvation was outside God's favor. Nothing anyone could say to you is worse than what the Lord has previously declared about you. Understanding this aspect of the gospel prevents you from fearing what others can say or do to you. Couple this gospel truth of what you were to whom you are in Christ, and you most assuredly have nothing to protect, fear, or hide (Romans 8:31–39). If you have been born again (John 3:7; Romans 10:9, 13), you are a child of the King—a person who has gone from the worst possible position that you could be to the best possible place you will ever know. If you are not living daily in this gospel truth, temptations will lure you toward insecurity that will motivate you to protect and defend your reputation before others. That kind of pride will truncate the effectiveness with which your friends can speak into your life—a soul-stunting posture before the Lord and others.

While the gospel is good news, its message also implies terrible news. You would not need the good news if there were no bad news. The same is true in Paul's progressive keys to Christian maturity that he laid out for his friend Timothy. Teaching brings reproof, which is supposed to knock us off our feet. That is the bad news. Thankfully, the Spirit of God would never leave us down and out (Psalm 23:3). He is the Healer who binds our wounds (Psalm 147:3). A careful and accurate rebuke from the Lord paves the way for His corrective measures that we can implement into our lives. The word "corrected" means to be stood up or made erect. God is a fixer. He does not rebuke us because He enjoys bringing pain into our lives. There is always a redemptive purpose for His corrections.

If the Lord does not convince you of this, you will be tentative about receiving reproof (Hebrews 12:6). Some will argue that they don't mind the rebukes of God, but it is the rebuke of sinful people that rubs them the wrong way. Horizontal soul care is a problem, for sure. It would be great if we perfectly rebuked people, but that is impossible among fallen creatures. Imperfect people reproving imperfect people will have an element of imperfection in it. Though there is a lot to say about wrongful rebukes, the point, for now, is whether we are mature enough and hungry enough to find the Lord's rebuke even through imperfect vessels. Can we learn anything from a poorly given rebuke? We can if our goal is Christian maturity. Maybe later, you can help the person who admonished you poorly.

Correction

- Are you more likely to focus on the reproof or the correction? (The former tends to be proud while the latter tends to be humble.)
- Are you more preoccupied with arguing with the "rebuker" or maturing in your sanctification for God's glory?
- Do you believe you need others to help you walk through sanctification issues?
- Do you enlist the help of your friends so that you can change?
- Do you believe others need you so you can help them walk through their sanctification issues?
- Would you say your commitment to change is more significant than your commitment to your reputation?

Righteous Training

Paul's four progressive and essential keys to change are:

1. **TEACHING:** "I want God's Word to teach me."
2. **REPROVING:** "As I learn from God's Word, I expect it to reprove me occasionally."
3. **CORRECTING:** "To be reproved is a door that leads to correction."
4. **TRAINING:** "After I'm corrected, I jump on God's training track where I can run my race more effectively." (See Hebrews 12:1 and 1 Corinthians 9:24–27.)

Each time you make it through steps one, two, and three, you will be ready to participate in ongoing training for righteous living. This process of progressive sanctification is not a one-and-done deal. These steps are recurring and unending until you see Jesus. Each day is a new opportunity to learn (teaching), fall (rebuke), get up (correction), and run a new way (training in righteousness). Imagine what it would be like if the Lord loved you enough to identify areas that could change your life daily. That kind of love invigorates the soul. Only Christians possess that kind of incremental, ongoing, unending, progressive path to freedom in Christ. Only Christians can change in long-term and sustainable ways. Imagine if the Lord saved you and left you to your former manner of life (Ephesians 4:22) with no way of changing—no chance to mature spiritually. Let's review!

1. **Teaching:** How often do you learn something from God's Word?
2. **Rebuke:** How often do you let the free conviction from the Spirit course through your mind?
3. **Correction:** How often do you benefit from His rerouting correctives?
4. **Training:** How often have you taken a new path to run your race for the Lord?

> He restores my soul. He leads me in paths of righteousness for his name's sake.
> (Psalm 23:3)

I recommend you teach your family and friends this template to help them mature in this progressive process. Invite them into your life growth plan. Appeal to them to come alongside you so you all can benefit from mutual and reciprocal gospel-shaped care. You're welcome to use my questions under each step. I recommend you add others along the way. Each person you meet with will add new insights, and the more you work through this template, you'll be the biggest winner. One of the best perks of my job is that I soak in sanctification truths every day, year in and year out. The more you teach, the more you'll learn and grow.

Two Traps

BAD EXPERIENCE: Some believers have had bad experiences with other Christians. In such cases, the temptation is to map their bad experience over what God could do redemptively in their lives. Sometimes a bad experience can be a person's worst enemy. It can also make you cynical about future grace, always thinking the worst about people's motives. Don't do that. Have faith in God (Hebrews 11:6). Let your faith in God's current process overcome the past evil that someone did to you. God's grace can outmaneuver and defeat bad experiences regardless of what they were.

ISOLATING YOURSELF: Don't isolate yourself from the community of faith. It is rare for a person to deteriorate in grace if they actively pursue gospel-shaped relationships. Isolation is the enemy's victory. We need loving and intentional friends interested in personal and practical exploration of life change. Most of the time, when I get in trouble, I isolate myself from the community. Sitting, soaking, and spectating on Sundays will not help you. You must engage God and others to change your life. Be open. Be honest. Be taught. Expect reproof, and anticipate correction, releasing you to run a spiritually productive race.

Call to Action

Will you work through the questions I have asked you in this chapter? It would benefit you if you brought along a friend for the journey. You can mutually encourage each other with some intentional and intrusive iron-sharpening conversations.

Ready?

Start running.

> Let us also lay aside every weight, and sin which clings so closely, and let us run with endurance the race that is set before us, looking to Jesus, the founder and perfecter of our faith, who for the joy that was set before him endured the cross, despising the shame, and is seated at the right hand of the throne of God.
>
> (Hebrews 12:1–2)

12

Marks of Change

What is the most trustworthy indicator of a person who has authentically changed? How can you know—as much as one can understand objective, practical transformation? "He said he changed, but did he?" Many folks have asked this question, and thankfully, Paul gives us our answers. But first, let me tell you a story. You know who they are: our friends, Biff and Mable, the couple who represent the best and worst of us. They make an excellent case study to help us see and understand authentic change in a person's life.

Biff and Mable

Sin had captured Biff, and after a season of struggle, he repented. But Mable was unsure if Biff truly changed because Biff did not appear to be different. He was not doing what he did before—praise God, but that was about it. Mable had a low-grade, gnawing anxiety that Biff would return to his old ways. It was not the first time he had "repented" of sin, so her hope for change was minimal as she fearfully guarded her heart. Understandably, she did not want to be hurt again, but it was also evident that she struggled as she placed less faith in God than in her husband's ability to stay changed.

Mable appealed, "If I could have assurances that he will not do it again. Is that too much to ask? Has he repented this time? Like, for real?" It's not too much to ask, but let me ask this: what is the most valid indicator of a person who has authentically changed? How can you know—as much as one can know—if a person is uncaught by sin? Paul gives us our answers in Ephesians. Let's take a look at his wise words, and then we can break them down to examine genuine repentance.

To put off your old self, which belongs to your former manner of life and is corrupt through deceitful desires, and to be renewed in the spirit of your minds, and to put on the new self, created after the likeness of God in true righteousness and holiness.
(Ephesians 4:22–24)

Old Out, New In

There are several things to consider from Paul's teaching, but I will only choose two: he was talking to Christians, and they had a former manner of life. Did you catch that? He talked to born-again, saved, regenerated, blood-bought, washed Christians who still struggled with temptations toward wicked, evil, sinful, and futile lives (Ephesians 4:17–22). They were saints tempted to shrink back and sin. Paul called those believers to put off their former manner of life—that lifestyle of unrighteousness seduces us to yield to moments of weakness.

He called them to walk no longer as the pagan Gentiles walked (Ephesians 4:17). Paul perceived the saint/sinner tension. He understood that Christians do sin (1 John 1:7–9), and he wanted to encourage them toward change (Romans 2:4). The implication for us is clear: we are not entirely sanctified, so Paul's teaching on transformation as a post-salvation Christian is helpful, leading to a few practical questions for our mutual self-examination.

- Are we daily putting off the old man?
- Are we actively renewing our inner man?
- Are we practically putting on a new lifestyle that is antithetically different from our former manner of life?

Paul informs us in the remaining verses what to look for in a genuinely changed person. Here is his sequential logic:

- Put off our former manner of life (22).
- Renew our inner man, the genesis of our sinfulness (23).
- Put on a new life like God—authentic right living and true holiness (24).

Change Illustrated

Paul did not want to leave us with an incomplete application of authentic right living and true holiness, which is what would have happened if he had stopped at Ephesians 4:24. We need more than conceptual language; we need functional language. Without application, we would have to speculate on the kind of repentance he asked us to put on. Fortunately, we will not have to guess. He gives four practical illustrations of what it means to authentically and effectually put off, renew, and put on a new lifestyle.

- **VERSE 25:** The lying person stops lying and begins to bless others with the truth.
- **VERSE 28:** The thief stops taking from individuals and becomes a proactive giver.
- **VERSE 29:** The corrupting talker ceases crude speech and builds up others with his tongue.
- **VERSE 31:** The harsh, bitter person puts away bitterness while spreading kindness to others.

Complete Change

One thing you perceive in this passage is that transformation is incomplete if we only stop doing bad things. You will know if repentance happened to someone by the proactive, practical, gospel-motivated blessings they provide to other people. Jesus did not come to earth to help us stop sinning. He had a higher vision. He wants us to go beyond the putting-off phase of our sanctification. Repentance is more than conceptual; it is practical. Actual repentance moves a person from selfishness to selflessness. Real change is long-term and sustained, others-centered living for the glory of God.

Note Paul's carefulness. He knew religious people could do good work. He used to be one of those religious people (Philippians 3:3–6), which is why he pressed the issue further. At the end of his practical application speech in verse 32, you see this as he wrapped up his entire argument for change by tying repentance directly to the gospel. Anyone can do good works; we call it behavioral modification, but only a person riveted to and motivated by the gospel can consistently glorify God through their works.

> Be kind to one another, tenderhearted, forgiving one another, as God in Christ forgave you.
> (Ephesians 4:32)

Gospel Connection

Paul connected our obedience to a gospel motive by saying, "As God in Christ forgave you." All work—regardless of what it may be—is motivated by something. Paul wanted to ensure he did not create nice-behaving Christians whose motives found motivation from something other than the gospel. Real change will find its motive rooted in the gospel of Jesus Christ. It will manifest as a penitent person actively living out the following five marks of attitudes and behaviors:

- **MARK ONE:** We are actively putting off our former manner of life (22).
- **MARK TWO:** We are actively renewing the spirit of our minds (23).
- **MARK THREE:** We actively pursue true righteousness and holiness (24).
- **MARK FOUR:** We actively and practically live out righteousness and holiness (25–32).
- **MARK FIVE:** The gospel motivates and sustains our behaviors (32).

Gospel Sustained

Paul's template for change has an aggressive quality, which is the opposite of the lukewarm Christian experience. Any Christianized person can somewhat do steps one through four and even appear to be changed based on observable behavior. A lack of gospel authenticity is why we must not miss Paul's gospel connection. If a person's heart motive is not rooted in the gospel, his behaviors will not last, no matter how good they may appear.

True righteousness and holiness flow from and find sustainability in the gospel—the person and work of Jesus Christ. I am not suggesting that you be a cynic or even suspicious of anyone who says they repented. The potential for change is not a call to be judgmental but a need to be discerning. It would be wrong to say, "Wait. We'll see if it's real or not." It would also be a mistake not to have humble and wise biblical expectations for practical transformation. Love believes all things and hopes all things, but love is not naive regarding Adamic tendencies (1 Corinthians 13:4–7).

Lack of Repentance

Let's say that Biff has not repented, and Mable is correct. It's possible. He artificially and temporarily put on a new self but retreated to his former manner of life shortly thereafter. In such a case, we want to examine why there is no sustainable change in Biff's life. Here are six possibilities that shed light on a person's lack of repentance, which should govern our hearts before we uncharitably judge someone because they have yet to change enough, or according to what we believe it should be.

1. **HE MAY NOT KNOW HOW TO REPENT:** Do not be surprised by this. Our children did not know how to repent when they were younger. I did not know how to repent until I became an adult. How many active and sin-engaging repenters do you know? Compare that number with how many Christians you know. I suspect there is a difference—a big difference. Not knowing how to change was the story of the Ethiopian eunuch. He had his Bible opened and in his lap but struggled to understand it. He needed to collaborate with someone (Acts 8:30-31). Some people talk about the Bible like it is a magic book. It is a powerful book, but it is not a magic book. In His wisdom, God chose the agency of humankind to cooperate with His Word and Spirit to help people change.

2. **AN ALLURING SIN MAY HAVE CAUGHT HIM:** While I am not dismissing personal responsibility for change, I am also not ignoring corporate responsibility. It takes a church. We are to be part of the process. Many Christians caught in sin do not know how to escape (Galatians 6:1). Caught people have difficulty repenting (James 1:14-15). Sin is alluring, and if a person has given most of his life over to satisfy his selfish desires, there is a possibility he will return to his sin. He needs our help.

3. **THE LORD IS MATURING MABLE:** Paul tells us to guard our hearts when helping people caught in sin (Galatians 6:1-2). If we do not protect our hearts, we will be culpable as we pile on someone else's sin. It is easy to sin against those we love, like when they do not change according to our timetable, expectations, desires, or agendas. The wise and humble person will ask, "What can I learn from this? What does the Lord want to teach me as I hope and pray for Biff's change?"

4. **THE LORD IS SUBMITTING MABLE TO HER CALLING:** Perchance Biff does not change. If so, she must remember her calling (1 Peter 2:21). The Lord's calling leads to death (Matthew 16:24). It could be the person you struggle the most with is God's kindness to you, as He uses that person to reorient your heart back to Him. The unchanging soul becomes an instrument of righteousness in the Lord's hands to mature you.

5. **WHAT YOU NEED WILL CONTROL YOU:** The thing we believe we need will control us, and we will know what rules us by how we respond to life's situations or the difficult people in our lives. When I sin against my wife, I believe I need whatever I am angry about, e.g., desires for love, appreciation, respect, or approval. If those things are where my heart is focused, not getting those things will cause me to respond sinfully to her. If I reorient my heart toward God, and if I am satisfied in Him alone, her behavior—good or bad—will have no ongoing control over me. If anyone other than God is controlling me, idolatry has captured me. My wife—at least for now—is being used by God to reveal my idolatry. God can use sin sinlessly, and

if I am sinning due to unmet expectations from another person, be sure to know Sovereign God is working for me by calling me to repentance.

6. **YOU MUST KNOW GOD IS GOOD:** Regardless of how this shakes out, Mable must be aware that God is good and that He is working in her life—even if she cannot perceive it. Moses could not have put up with the shenanigans of Pharaoh if he was not "in faith," believing God was working out something good for him and others. His faith was rooted in God alone, and ours must be too. Repentance is a tricky thing, and the truth is that we cannot ultimately tell if anyone has authentically changed. Repentance is God's responsibility to grant (2 Timothy 2:25). Our responsibility is to rest in His sovereign care over our lives. If our affection is in God alone, we will be okay regardless of what others do.

Call to Action

1. Do you know how to repent fully? Can you break down the process?
2. Are you part of a church that is humbly transparent about its sin struggles?
3. Are you a humble and compassionate friend to your struggling friends?
4. How are you maturing in Christ through the struggles of your friends?
5. Based on your responses to your complicated relationships, what would you say controls you?

Conclusion

Warning and Blessing

Therefore, as the Holy Spirit says, "Today, if you hear his voice, do not harden your hearts as in the rebellion, on the day of testing in the wilderness, where your fathers put me to the test and saw my works for forty years. Therefore I was provoked with that generation, and said, 'They always go astray in their heart; they have not known my ways.' As I swore in my wrath, 'They shall not enter my rest.'" Take care, brothers, lest there be in any of you an evil, unbelieving heart, leading you to fall away from the living God. But exhort one another every day, as long as it is called "today," that none of you may be hardened by the deceitfulness of sin.

(Hebrews 3:7–13)

Do You Hear?

Did the Spirit of God illuminate you at any point as you were reading this book? How did you respond to Him? How should you respond to Him? This book is a working document; it does not read like a novel. Each chapter is an opportunity to digest, process, reflect, and practice. If you have read it as such, you have already experienced change. The presence

Conclusion

of change is working in you. Be encouraged. Also, consider rereading it. Slower. Maybe it would benefit you if you went through this book with a friend. A small group format could be invigorating, revealing, and transformative.

Finally, will you write me if the LORD has done a good thing in you? Let me know about His gracious work in your life. I would find no greater joy than to hear how you're walking in His truth (3 John 1:4).

Rick

About the Author

Rick Thomas launched the Life Over Coffee global training network in 2008 to bring hope and help for you and others by creating resources that spark conversations for transformation. His primary responsibilities are resource creation and leadership development, which he does through speaking, writing, podcasting, and educating. In 1990 he earned a BA in Theology and, in 1991, a BS in Education. In 1993, he received his ordination into Christian ministry, and in 2000, he graduated with an MA in Counseling from The Master's University. In 2006, he was recognized as a Fellow of the Association of Certified Biblical Counselors (ACBC).

Other Books Available from Life Over Coffee

Boasting in Weakness
Centering Your Marriage on Christ
Communication
Complete Marriage
Don't Apologize
Exchange the Truth for a Lie
Help My Marriage Has Grown Cold
Identity Crisis
Local Church
Loving Me
Mad
Marriage Devotion We Are One
Politics and Culture
Parenting Devotion from Zero to Adulthood
Sex, Temptation, and Modesty
Storm Hurler
The Cyber Effect
The Talk
Wives Leading
You Decide

www.ingramcontent.com/pod-product-compliance
Lightning Source LLC
Chambersburg PA
CBHW052146070526
44585CB00017B/2005